M000278929

# TURNING ON THE LIGHT

## Discovering the Riches of God's Word

Carol J. Ruvolo

P&R PUBLISHING
P.O. BOX 817 • PHILLIPSBURG • NEW JERSEY 08865-0817

Unless otherwise indicated, Scripture quotations are from the New
American Standard Bible. Copyright by the Lockman Foundation
1960, 1962, 1963, 1968, 1971, 1973, 1975, 1977. Italics indicate
emphasis added.

Printed in the United States of America

*Composition by Colophon Typesetting*

**Library of Congress Cataloging-in-Publication Data**

Ruvolo, Carol J., 1946–
    Turning on the light : discovering the riches of God's Word /
Carol J. Ruvolo.
        p.   cm. — (Light for your path)
    Includes bibliographical references.
    ISBN 0-87552-626-8 (pbk.)
        1. Bible—Study and teaching. 2. Christian women—Religious life.
I. Title. II. Series.
BS600.2.R88   1998
220´.071—dc21                                            98-14475

# TURNING ON THE LIGHT

# Light for Your Path

The Light for Your Path Series is for women who desire to know, love, and serve God better. Each book is designed to nurture new believers while challenging women who are ready for deeper study. Studies in the series examine *books* of the Bible, on the one hand (look for subtitles beginning with *Light from*), and important *topics* in Christian faith and life, on the other (look for subtitles beginning with *Focus on*). The series blends careful instruction with active reader participation in a variety of study exercises, always encouraging women to live in the light of biblical truth in practical ways.

Two foundational studies explain why and how to study the Bible as the one perfect light source for your Christian walk:

*A Book Like No Other: What's So Special About the Bible*
*Turning On the Light: Discovering the Riches of God's Word*

*To the women of the*
*Thursday morning*
*Bible study:*

| | |
|---|---|
| *Blair* | *Brenda* |
| *Carol* | *Diana* |
| *Elaine* | *Janet* |
| *Juanita* | *Linno* |
| *Maria* | *Marilyn* |

*Beautiful examples of how*
*iron sharpens iron.*
*God bless you every one!*

# CONTENTS

*Contents*

# The Light for Your Path Series

The Light for Your Path Series is designed to help women learn how to glorify and enjoy God by living out their transformation in Christ. Each book in the series reflects the author's commitment to the Bible as the infallible, inerrant, authoritative, and entirely sufficient Word of God, and her conviction that Reformed theology is the clearest and most accurate restatement of biblical truth.

The series begins with two foundational studies centering on the Bible itself. *A Book Like No Other: What's So Special About the Bible* presents (in six lessons) the unique character of God's revelation. *Turning On the Light: Discovering the Riches of God's Word* provides (in seven lessons) an effective approach to studying the Bible. Combining these two books in a thirteen-week course will prepare new and veteran students to gain the most from the Light for Your Path Series.

The remaining studies in the series fall into two categories. "Light" studies cover particular *books* of the Bible (or sections of books, or groups of books such as the Gospels). These studies guide you through portions of Scripture, enabling you to understand and apply the meaning of each passage. You will recognize them by their subtitles, beginning with the words *Light from.*

"Focus" studies spotlight important *topics* in the Christian faith and life, such as prayer, salvation, righteousness, and relationships, and seek to show what the whole Bible says about them. These studies also stress understanding and applying biblical truth in daily life. Their subtitles begin with the words *Focus on.* The *Leader's Guide* that accompanies this series contains a complete description of the purpose and format of these studies, along with helpful suggestions for leading women through them.

Studying a combination of biblical books and topics will shed much-needed scriptural light on your walk with God. Both types of Bible study should be included in a "balanced diet" for a growing Christian.

Bible study is a serious task that involves a significant investment of time and energy. Preparing yourself to study effectively will help you reap the greatest benefit from that investment. Study when you are well rested and alert. Try to find a time and place that is quiet, free of distractions, and conducive to concentration. Use a loose-leaf or spiral notebook to take notes on what you read and to do the exercises in this study. You may also want to develop a simple filing system so that you can refer to these notes in later studies.

Approach Bible study as you would any task that requires thought and effort to do well. Don't be surprised if it challenges you and stretches your thinking. Expect it to be difficult at times but extremely rewarding.

Always begin your study with prayer. Ask the Lord to reveal sin in your life that needs to be confessed and cleansed, to help you concentrate on His truths, and to illumine your mind with understanding of what He has written. End your study with a prayer for opportunities to apply what you have learned and wisdom to recognize those opportunities when they occur.

Each lesson in these studies is followed by three types of "Exercises": "Review," "Application," and "Digging Deeper." The *review* exercises will help you determine how well you understood the lesson material by giving you an opportunity to express the key points in your own words. The *application* exercises encourage you to put your understanding of the material to work in your daily life. And the *digging deeper* exercises challenge you to pursue further study in certain key areas.

You should be able to find the answers to the *review* exercises in the lesson material itself, but please resist the temptation to copy words or phrases out of the lesson when you answer these questions. Work at putting these ideas into your own words. When you can do this, you know you have understood what you have read.

It might help to ask yourself, "How would I explain this idea to someone else if I didn't have the book with me?"

If you don't have time to do all of the *application* exercises, pray over them and ask the Lord to show you which one(s) *He* wants you to work on. Because you will be applying the lessons to your daily life, these applications should take some time and thought. Answering one of them well will benefit you more than answering all of them superficially.

Answers to the application exercises should be very specific. Work at avoiding vague generalities. It might help to keep in mind that a specific application will answer the questions Who? What? When? Where? and How? A vague generality will not. You can make applications in the areas of your thinking, your attitudes, and your behavior. (See lesson 6 of *Turning On the Light* for more about application.)

*Digging deeper* exercises usually require a significant amount of time and effort to complete. They were designed to provide a challenge for mature Christians who are eager for more advanced study. However, new Christians should not automatically pass them by. The Holy Spirit may choose to use one of them to help you grow. Remember that *all Christians* grow by stretching beyond where they are right now. So if one or two of these exercises intrigue you, spend some time working on them. And, do not hesitate to ask for help from your pastor, elders, or more mature Christian friends.

As you work through this study, resist the temptation to compare yourself with other Christians in your group. The purpose of this study is to help you grow in your faith by learning and applying God's truth in your daily life—not to fill up a study book with brilliantly worded answers. If you learn and apply *one element* of God's truth in each lesson, you are consistently moving beyond where you were when you began.

Always remember that effective Bible study equips you *to glorify God and enjoy Him forever.* You glorify God when you live in such a way that those around you can look at you and see an accurate reflection of God's character and nature. You enjoy God when you are fully satisfied in His providential ordering of the circumstances in your life. When your life glorifies God and your joy is rooted in His providence, your impact on our fallen world will be tremendous.

# ACKNOWLEDGMENTS

Many years ago, a committed Navigator named D. J. Warren invested a great deal of time and effort in discipling me. She started at "square one" and patiently taught me, by word and example, how to strive to walk worthy of my high calling in Jesus Christ.

One of the lessons I learned at her dining-room table was that God never calls us to a task without also fully equipping us for the job (2 Corinthians 9:8). Since that time, I have learned that God's work of equipping us for ministry includes sending gifted brothers and sisters to help us accomplish the good works He has prepared for us to do.

Many cherished brothers and sisters have come alongside me to help bring *Turning On the Light* into being. The WIC Council of Providence Presbyterian Church in Albuquerque suggested the idea of a Reformed Bible study for women and graciously asked me to try my hand at writing it. Those ladies (Juanita Chiu, Blair Willis, Janet Moffatt, and Carol Meyers) listened to my ideas, made suggestions, and enthusiastically supported the project.

The elders and deacons at Providence read the drafts, made more suggestions, approved the study, and encouraged me to start looking for a publisher. Those men (Randy Steele, Rick Davidson, John Linebarger, Gary Westerfield, and John Wallace) challenged me to think carefully and write cogently, and refused to let me quit.

The ladies of the Thursday morning Bible study (to whom the study is dedicated) labored through the material, not only as eager Bible students but also as extremely constructive critics, seeking out typographical errors, incoherent sentences, and questionable questions. Their diligent attention to detail was absolutely invaluable.

My mother, Betty Boling, and her dear friends, Jake and Barbara Bailey, Elsie Newell, and Elaine Kent, have encouraged my writing efforts for more years than I care to think about. Their loyal, albeit understandably less than objective, support has rejuvenated me again and again, and I don't know what I would do without them.

The people at P&R Publishing, particularly Barbara Lerch and Thom Notaro, have patiently guided me through the bewildering maze of Christian publishing with incredible skill and delightful tactfulness. It has been a joy to work with these outstanding professionals.

My husband, Frank, and my daughter, Cinnamon, continue to demonstrate the beauty of their unflappable natures by gracefully adjusting their lives to the inevitable vicissitudes of life with a writer mom. They never complain but simply pick up and deal with an incalculable number of familial loose ends I never seem to get around to. What a blessing they are!

To everyone who had a part in this work, I extend my heartfelt gratitude. May our gracious Lord be pleased to use this offering to equip His people for the work of service and thereby glorify Himself.

*With the right of private interpretation*
*comes the sober responsibility*
*of accurate interpretation. Private interpretation*
*gives us license to interpret, not distort.*
*—R. C. Sproul*

# The Letter

"*Why* *didn't I just make two trips to the car?*" *Susan fumed, fumbling with her keys while precariously juggling her purse, tote bag, and the hastily retrieved contents of her overflowing mailbox.*

*"Because it's raining and you just had your hair done, that's why," she answered herself as the uncooperative key finally slid home, allowing her to push open the heavy oak door. Barely across the threshold, she glimpsed a familiar reddish-brown blur bounding toward her and lost her grip on the mail in a futile attempt to ward off a typically over-eager greeting from her exuberant Irish Setter.*

*"Hey, Lucy, did you miss me?" She laughed as she turned her face away from an onslaught of sloppy welcome-home kisses and gently pushed the dog away. "Sit, Lucy," she commanded, stooping to retrieve the mail now scattered over most of her living room rug. "Look at what you did!"*

*Undaunted by her owner's chiding remarks, Lucy squirmed happily and thumped her tail on the floor while Susan scurried around picking up letters and packages.*

*She deposited the stack of mail on the table by the door and sighed, suddenly realizing how tired she was. "What a day," she groaned, rubbing her eyes and turning back to the waiting dog. "C'mon, Lucy, you wanna go outside?" Lucy bolted for the back door, and Susan followed with considerably less enthusiasm.*

*About halfway across the room, she spied the corner of an overlooked envelope peeking out from beneath the sofa and bent to retrieve it. Instantly recognizing the elegant handwriting adorning the deli-*

*cate pink stationary, she felt her fatigue begin to melt away as she eagerly tore open the envelope.*

*Lucy's impatient whining prompted Susan to read the letter outside,.and she followed the dog into the yard with a lighter step and brighter eyes. "Celia," she smiled as she thought of her best friend now far away. "Oh, how much I have needed to hear from you!"*

*For the next twenty minutes, as the sky cleared, she savored the letter, practically oblivious to everything around her. She read it once quickly and then again more slowly, relishing every detail of her friend's adventures in a distant land, and luxuriating in the comforting between-the-lines assurances of their enduring soul mate relationship.*

—  —  —

A letter from a friend. What a welcome intrusion in our typically hectic schedules. How we love to call intermission in the game of life, sink into a cozy chair with those newly received pages filled with familiar script, and revel in the joys of friendship.

I don't think I ever fully appreciated the value of a friend's letter until the day my best friend left for Germany. We had developed an extremely close relationship in a relatively short time and were both heartbroken by the prospects of a separation that might last ten years or more. We promised each other we wouldn't cry, and we didn't. (At least not until we were out of each other's sight.) And we promised each other we would write . . . and we did.

We wrote letters, we sent cards, we even recorded audio and video tapes and mailed them to each other. During the ensuing seven years her address changed four times while mine remained the same, and we have now reluctantly accepted the fact that we may never again live in the same city; however, our friendship is still strong.

We have shared our joys and heartaches; and when one of us has fallen, the other has been quick to lift up her companion. She is my friend, my soul mate, my cherished correspondent. I love hearing from her. I stop the world to read her letters. They are truly a welcome intrusion in my typically hectic schedule.

But as much as I treasure her letters, there is another letter I treasure more. It's the Letter from my Father—the one He wrote to tell me about His love for me, His plans for me, and His requirements for me. It's a Letter written in the blood of His beloved Son—the Son who died so that I could live, the Son who willingly bore my Father's wrath against my sin, the Son who is now preparing a place for me in eternity. It's a Letter whose pages are stained with tears and worn from repeated readings. It's a Letter that is sometimes difficult to understand and demands my best efforts to absorb its full meaning.

It consumes my thoughts, controls my behavior, and establishes my priorities. It never changes and never grows stale. It is dynamically alive and constantly challenges me to reach beyond my own limitations toward my Father's perfection. It's a Letter I will never grow tired of reading because it comes from the heart of my Father who knows me better than I know myself and loves me in spite of what He knows.

## The Challenge of Serious Bible Study

If you are a Christian, you too have good reason to treasure God's Letter to you, the Bible. Your Father chose you from before the foundation of the world to work toward the accomplishment of His purposes and goals. To make sure you understand your part in those purposes and goals, He revealed in His Letter to you everything you need to live according to His plan.

What a joyous privilege to have such a unique Letter in your possession! As you read it, study it, and act on it, you will find your relationship with its Author growing deeper and stronger than you ever thought possible—and your life will begin to reflect His glory in a way that will have great impact on those around you. The Letter is worth your best effort—the effort we have called "serious Bible study."

Serious Bible study encompasses specific prerequisites, techniques, and objectives. The *prerequisites* are (1) having an accurate view of the Letter and (2) having an accurate view of yourself. The *techniques* are (1) accurately observing what the Letter says, (2) responsibly interpreting what the Letter means, and (3) meaningfully applying the Letter's teachings to your life. The *goals* are

(1) becoming conformed to the image of your Lord Jesus Christ, (2) glorifying your heavenly Father, and (3) learning to do the work your Father prepared for you to do.

The first two lessons of this study deal with the prerequisites of serious Bible study, the next four deal with the techniques, and the last lesson deals with the objectives.

As you work through the lessons, I hope you will catch the excitement of the challenge. Your Father's commands are never burdensome and were given in love to provide you with abundant life. As you learn to walk worthy of your calling, may you be filled with joy as you watch your Father do exceedingly abundantly beyond all that you ask or think according to the power that works within you.

# LESSON 1

# Special Delivery

*People study the Bible for many reasons, not all of which honor the God who wrote it. That's why our study begins with two lessons on relating correctly to God's Word. Before we can glorify God through the study of His Book, we must understand some things about that Book and about ourselves. Lesson 1 will help us understand the Book, and lesson 2 will help us understand ourselves.*

The Bible was written for the purpose of revelation. As fallen human beings we would never have known the truth about God if He had not chosen to reveal Himself to us. Without God's revelation of Himself to us, we would have been left to create Him in our image—which is exactly how every man-generated religion in the world originated.

God didn't have to reveal Himself to us. He would have been perfectly justified in leaving us to our futile speculations about His existence and purposes, but He chose instead to graciously shed the light of His glory into our darkened hearts and minds.

## *A Double Dose of Revelation*

God reveals Himself to us in two ways: *natural revelation* and *special revelation*. Israel's King David and the church's apostle Paul describe natural revelation for us.

> The heavens are telling of the glory of God;
> And their expanse is declaring the work of His hands.
> (Psalm 19:1)

> For since the creation of the world His invisible attributes, His eternal power and divine nature, have been clearly seen, being understood through what has been made, so that they are without excuse. (Romans 1:20)

*Natural revelation* tells us that God exists and that He created the universe in which we live.[1] It tells us that God is powerful, orderly, and purposeful, but it tells us nothing about the way He relates to His creation. Natural revelation testifies to the magnitude and quality of the Creator's handiwork but it reveals nothing about His heart. It doesn't tell us whether God created us on a whim and left us to fend for ourselves or is actively involved in running the universe. It doesn't tell us whether God likes us, requires anything of us, or has any plans for us. As created beings, we can only know His personality, mind, and motives if He chooses to speak to us. And speak He has—through His special revelation!

*Special revelation* is commonly referred to as God's *Word*. The Old Testament tells us that God's Word came to the patriarchs and prophets (Genesis 15:1; Numbers 36:5; Deuteronomy 18:20–22; Joshua 8:27; 14:6; 1 Samuel 3:1; 15:10; 2 Samuel 7:4; 1 Kings 18:1; Isaiah 38:4; 55:11; Jeremiah 1:4; Ezekiel 7:1; Daniel 9:2; Hosea 1:1; Joel 1:1; Amos 3:1; Jonah 1:1; Micah 1:1; Zephaniah 1:1; Haggai 1:1; Zechariah 1:1).

God spoke to the men He had specially chosen and equipped to communicate His truth to His people. He told them who He was and what His requirements were. He also told them who they were and what they could expect of Him. He told them much of what He was planning for the future but left them wondering about many things.

The New Testament contains the record of God's Word made flesh in Jesus Christ. John 1:1, 14 tells us, "In the beginning was the Word, and the Word was with God, and the Word was God. . . . And the Word became flesh, and dwelt among us, and we beheld His glory, glory as of the only begotten from the Father, full of grace and truth."

Jesus Christ is the epitome of special revelation because He is the "image of the invisible God" and "the exact representation of His nature" (Colossians 1:15; Hebrews 1:3). He assured His disciple Philip, "He who has seen Me has seen the Father" (John 14:9), and shocked the Jews by declaring, "I and the Father are one" (John 10:30). It is only through Jesus that we come to know the Father. "No one comes to the Father, but through Me" (John 14:6).

## The Theme of the Bible Is Jesus

Jesus is the focus of God's special revelation to us. The entire Bible centers on His work of redemption. Daniel M. Doriani, in his book *Getting the Message,* says, "Every passage in the Bible presents Christ both as the remedy for human fallenness and as the end point of God's plan of salvation."[2]

Humanity's fall into sin cast us into a pit of suffering. All of us have experienced firsthand the painful effects of sin. We suffer when we sin and when other people sin. We suffer because we live in a cursed world that lies in the grip of the Evil One. And we suffer the effects of ignorance—clouded thinking produced by worldly wise fallen fools.

The Bible portrays a threefold remedy in Jesus Christ for the suffering that was unleashed in the Fall. (1) The redemptive work of Christ on the cross not only paid the penalty of sin, it effectively broke sin's power to control the redeemed. Romans 6 describes Christians as those who were once slaves to sin but are now free from its mastery. (2) Jesus' second coming in judgment will restore the natural world to its original glorious splendor. Romans 8 and Revelation 20 describe the future liberation of the created order from its cursed corruption when the Prince of This World is overthrown. (3) Our Lord's transforming work of regeneration also renews believer's minds. First Corinthians 2:16 and Romans 12:1

describe the transformation of arrogant fallen fools into humble possessors of the mind of Christ.

Jesus can be seen as the remedy for human suffering only because the Bible presents Him as the focal point of God's eternal plan of redemption. Even though suffering is not eliminated in redemption, it takes on a whole new meaning when viewed from the perspective of God's redemptive history. Every page of the Bible uses human suffering as a backdrop to demonstrate the need, the accomplishment, and the consequences of redemption in Jesus Christ.

The first five books of the Old Testament (the Pentateuch) describe the entry of sin into God's perfect world and God's reaction to that event. Man jumped at the opportunity to disregard God's Word, and God responded by condemning man and nature to live with the consequences of disobedience. He established His law as an unwavering standard of perfection and established the system of Old Testament sacrifices to remind His people of their sinful disregard of His Word. But He also promised them a Redeemer—One who would be the only means of overcoming their sin-induced weakness and rebellion.

The Historical Books of the Old Testament vividly describe humanity's preference for self-glorification and God's refusal to give His glory to another. God's chosen people persisted in doing what was right in their own eyes. Not content to demonstrate God's righteousness by separating themselves from their worldly neighbors, they chose to imitate the sinful lifestyles of those around them by flirting with their neighbor's gods and mimicking their political system. The cosmic conflict between the seed of the woman and the seed of the Serpent is clearly evident in the downward spiral of Israel's history from the glorious crowning of King Saul to the crushing disgrace of the Captivity.

The Prophetic Books call God's people to covenant obedience and love for God. They also warn of the consequences of disobedience and promise mercy through the work of the coming Messiah. The Wisdom Literature of the Old Testament lays bare the depravity of the human heart and establishes the source of true wisdom in Jesus Christ.

The Old Testament sets the stage for the entrance of the Redeemer in the Gospels. The four gospel writers portray Jesus as King, Prophet, Priest, Teacher, Son of God, Son of Man, and as the true Israelite who alone kept God's covenant perfectly. As all these things, He fulfilled all of God's requirements and bore His righteous wrath against sin so that the elect could be forgiven and become the object of God's gracious mercy.

Paul's Epistles explain in great detail how Jesus' life, work, death, and resurrection atone for sin, grant forgiveness, and restore a right relationship with God. The epistle to the Hebrews portrays Jesus as the absolute High Priest and perfect sacrifice who decisively defeats Satan, while the book of Revelation presents a series of visions of Christ in His triumph over Satan and his allies.

The New Testament books written by Peter, John, James, and Jude round out our necessary knowledge of Jesus by digging into issues of ethics, endurance, and assurance, while the book of Acts describes our glorious heritage in the church.

## The Validity of the Biblical Record

If the Bible was indeed written by God for the purpose of revealing His truth to us, it must be trustworthy. A book written by God would have to be infallible, inerrant, and sufficiently useful to meet our needs. It would also have to be absolutely irrefutable, indisputable, and indispensable.[3]

The Bible boldly declares all these things about itself. It claims divine authorship. It does not claim to be just another book or a compilation of various human attempts to define God and His work. The Bible leaves us only two alternatives when we read it: accept it as God's Word to us, or reject it as a poorly crafted fraud.[4]

Second Timothy 3:16–17 says, "All Scripture is inspired by God and profitable for teaching, for reproof, for correction, for training in righteousness; that the man of God may be adequate, equipped for every good work." Paul wrote these words to his spiritual son Timothy from a Roman prison where he was awaiting execution. They were included in a letter full of encouragement and instruction. Paul's race had been run; he had fought the good fight, finished the course, and kept the faith; and he was looking forward to receiving his rewards.

Timothy's race, however, was just beginning. He was facing the daunting prospect of stepping into the great apostle's oversized shoes and was scared to death. He needed all the encouragement and instruction he could get! Paul understood Timothy's need and expended a great deal of his final energies building up his beloved successor. One of the things he told Timothy to remember was that his life and ministry must be based solidly on the Word of God. Everything he said and did in service to God had to rest upon the revealed truth of Scripture.

He reminds Timothy of two essential elements of God's Word: (1) *All* of it is *inspired* by God, and (2) *all* of it is *profitable*. Paul would not have agreed with modern scholars who try to ignore uncomfortable passages of Scripture by teaching that the Bible merely *contains* the Word of God and that it is up to us to determine what is inspired and what is not. He affirmed the Bible's complete inspiration.

The Greek word translated "inspired" literally means "breathed out." Louis Berkhof defines inspiration as "that supernatural influence exerted on the sacred writers by the Holy Spirit by virtue of which their writings are given divine truthfulness, and constitute an infallible and sufficient rule of faith and practice."[5] Paul's apostolic companion Peter describes it this way: "But know this first of all, that no prophecy of Scripture is a matter of one's own interpretation, for no prophecy was ever made by an act of human will, but men moved by the Holy Spirit spoke from God" (2 Peter 1:20–21).

Because the Bible is inspired ("breathed out" by God), it is *profitable*. And Paul tells Timothy it is profitable for four things: *teaching, reproof, correction,* and *training in righteousness.*

*Teaching* is another word for doctrine and refers to the body of truth recorded in Scripture. We cannot begin to glorify God and live according to His requirements until we know who He is and what He requires. The Bible teaches us those things.

*Reproof* is rebuke that is closely aligned with the legal concept of conviction. Reproof accurately asserts that the charges brought against a sinner are true and accurate. We stand before the Word of God guilty as charged. We have been confronted with God's truths in the form of teaching and have seen how far short of their requirements we have fallen. Our response to reproof should be repentance—a desire to turn from sin to righteousness demonstrated by a willingness to make practical changes in our lives.

*Correction* facilitates repentance by helping us carry out godly changes in our lives. Scripture corrects us by showing us how to flee from sin in the pursuit of righteousness. It prevents reproof from becoming a morbid exercise in futile introspection by turning it into a springboard to godliness.

*Training in righteousness* could be referred to as spiritual discipline. Training in righteousness takes what we have learned from teaching, reproof, and correction and applies it to specific areas of our lives. It happens when the things we have learned in the pages of God's Word affect the way we think, speak, and act.

Teaching, reproof, correction, and training in righteousness *equip* us *adequately* to serve God. The word *adequate* in modern usage sometimes carries the idea of barely sufficient, but the Greek word used here means capable and proficient. The word *equipped* means thoroughly fitted, and is used to refer to a ship fully rigged out for a voyage.

Ephesians 2:10 tells us that we were "created in Christ Jesus for good works, which God prepared beforehand, that we should walk in them." It is the teaching, reproving, correcting, and training qualities of God's holy Word that equip us to adequately carry out our created purpose.

## Notes

1. Space does not permit a detailed discussion of the existence of God and His work of Creation. If you are still questioning the existence of God, you should not continue this study until you have settled that issue in your own mind. I would recommend you start by reading *Mere Christianity* by C. S. Lewis. If you would like to pursue the study of God's work of creation, you would greatly benefit by reading Henry Morris's books, particularly *The Genesis Record* and *The Long War Against God,* and R. C. Sproul's, *Not A Chance.*

2. Daniel M. Doriani, *Getting the Message: A Plan for Interpreting and Applying the Bible* (Phillipsburg, N.J.: P&R Publishing, 1996), 171. I am deeply indebted to Dr. Doriani's analysis of the "fallen-condition focus" and the "redemptive-historical focus" in chapter 12 of his book.

3. This study assumes that participating students have already been convinced of the authoritative truthfulness of the Bible. If you are not yet sure that the Bible is the infallible, inerrant Word of God, please do not continue until you have settled this issue in your own mind. A good place to start would be Josh McDowell, *Evidence That Demands a Verdict.*

4. For more information on this subject, see C. S. Lewis, *Mere Christianity.*

5. Louis Berkhof, *Principles of Biblical Interpretation* (Grand Rapids: Baker, 1950), 41.

## *Exercises*

### *Review*

1. List several specific reasons why you think it is important to study the Bible.

2. Explain the difference between natural and special revelation.

3. In your own words, explain why Jesus is the epitome of special revelation.

4. How do Jesus' life and work relate to human suffering?

5. Study 1 Corinthians 2:12–16, 2 Corinthians 10:5, and Romans 12:1–2, and explain what it means to "have the mind of Christ."

6. In your own words, define "inspiration." How does it differ from revelation?

7. Describe each of the four ways God's Word is profitable to us. Then describe a personal experience in which the Word of God adequately equipped you to minister in some way. In your description, point out how you were taught, reproved, corrected, and trained by Scripture.

## *Application*

1. Read and meditate on Psalm 19:7–14, and complete the following chart describing God's Word:

| GOD'S WORD | IS (ARE) | DOES (DO) |
|---|---|---|
| law of the Lord | perfect | restores the soul |
| testimony of the Lord | | |
| precepts of the Lord | | |
| commandment of the Lord | | |
| fear of the Lord | | |
| judgments of the Lord | | |
| they (v. 10) | | |
| them (v. 11) | | |

What additional information do you learn about God's Word from verses 12–14?

2. See if you can relate Psalm 19:7–14 to 2 Timothy 3:16–17 by placing each description of Scripture found in Psalm 19:7–14 in one or more of the following "categories of usefulness" found in 2 Timothy 3:16–17:

teaching (instruction):
rebuke:
correction:
training in righteousness:

How might understanding Psalm 19:7–14 in the light of 2 Timothy 3:16–17 equip you to serve God more effectively?

3. Christianity has always had large percentages of women in its ranks—women whom God has used greatly to further His kingdom through their impact on their families, their neighborhoods, and their world. However, relatively few Christian women have accepted the challenge of serious Bible study, and many of their reasons for not doing so are represented below:

**Sylvia's reason:**

"Frankly, I don't have the time. With four children under the age of ten and a husband who works fifty hours a week, I'm lucky to get a few minutes a day to read a few verses and say a quick prayer. Maybe when the children are older . . . but right now, serious Bible study is out of the question."

**Lynda's reason:**

"My husband is the head of our house and my high priest. He does all the Bible study and determines what our family will believe. My job is to follow his lead without question and support his decisions. Studying the Bible on my own would only confuse me and make it harder for me to follow his leadership."

**Stephanie's reason:**

"I read the Bible every day and it means so much to me. I experience the most wonderful feelings of peace and contentment when I read God's Word, and I don't want to lose that. I am afraid if I start studying the Bible like a subject in school, it will become nothing more than an academic exercise instead of the profound emotional experience it is now."

**Tanya's reason:**

"I go to a wonderful church and my pastor has spent years studying the Bible. He is a truly gifted teacher who explains the Bible so well. I know I could never study the Bible as well as he does, so I am content to just let him teach me."

**Cynthia's reason:**
"I would like to, but I have no idea how to do it."

**Rita's reason:**
"I'm not sure the Bible is reliable. Some of those stories are pretty fantastic and sound more like myths and fairy tales than facts, and I'm not one to base my life on myths and fairy tales."

**Karin's reason:**
"I do study the Bible, and I love it. I'm just not sure I am coming up with the right answers. There are so many Bible teachers and scholars who disagree on what different parts of the Bible mean. How do I know I am believing the right things?"

**Helen's reason:**
"Jesus is my Savior and He is all I need. I pray every day and listen for His voice. I depend on the Holy Spirit to guide me in everything I do. The Bible doesn't speak to me the way His Spirit does, so I don't pay much attention to it."

**Diana's reason:**
"I used to study the Bible, and I felt guilty all the time. It got to where I couldn't take it anymore, and I feel much better since I quit."

How would you respond to each of these women if you had the opportunity to encourage them to accept the challenge of serious Bible study?

Sylvia:
Lynda:
Stephanie:
Tanya:
Cynthia:
Rita:

Karin:
Helen:
Diana:

Are *you* ready to accept the challenge of serious Bible study? Why or why not?

## Digging Deeper

1. Is natural revelation sufficient to bring a person to salvation? Why or why not? Support your reasoning with Scripture.

2. If Jesus is the solution to suffering, why do Christians continue to suffer after they are saved? Support your answer with Scripture.

3. How would you defend your belief in the Bible as God's authoritative Word if someone challenged you to explain how you could believe anything so ridiculous? (Read 1 Peter 3:13–17 and allow it to shape the *attitude* behind your answer.)

4. Trace the portrayal of Jesus as the focal point of God's eternal plan of redemption through the Bible. Be as creative as you can here. Try your hand at a poem, a song, a diagram, or a picture. Think about how you might present this truth to a child, someone of a different culture, or someone challenged by a learning disability.

# LESSON 2
# Handle with Care

*In lesson 1, we learned that the Bible was written by God for the purpose of revelation. In it, God tells us what we need to know in order to serve Him honorably. When we open the Bible, we approach the throne of God. We should never do this casually or selfishly, but reverently, respectfully, and humbly. Developing the attitudes necessary for effective Bible study requires some effort, and lesson 2 will help us prepare ourselves to "draw near with confidence to the throne of grace, that we may receive mercy and may find grace to help in time of need" (Hebrews 4:16).*

Twentieth-century Christianity is distressingly man-centered. Most of our modern religious activities center on meeting people's needs rather than exalting God. We allow ourselves to become so preoccupied with the *activities* of ministry that we lose sight of its *purpose*. We need to remind ourselves of our Savior's example. While Jesus walked this earth, He occupied Himself with the activities of ministry, but He never lost sight of His ministry's purpose. Everything Jesus did pointed people to God. Meeting people's needs was not the focal point of His ministry; He met people's needs as a *means* of opening their hearts to God. And He left instructions for us to do the same.

## The Right Focus

In the second chapter of Philippians, Paul underscores the value of meeting other people's needs when he admonishes us to "do nothing from selfishness or empty conceit, but with humility of mind let each of you regard one another as more important than himself; do not merely look out for your own personal interests, but also for the interests of others" (vv. 3–4). However, he set that admonition in a context we dare not ignore.

> If therefore there is any encouragement in Christ, if there is any consolation of love, if there is any fellowship of the Spirit, if any affection and compassion, make my joy complete by being of the same mind, maintaining the same love, united in spirit, intent on one purpose.
>
> Do nothing from selfishness or empty conceit, but with humility of mind let each of you regard one another as more important than himself; do not merely look out for your own personal interests, but also for the interests of others.
>
> Have this attitude in yourselves which was also in Christ Jesus, who, although He existed in the form of God, did not regard equality with God a thing to be grasped, but emptied Himself, taking the form of a bond-servant, and being made in the likeness of men. And being found in appearance as a man, He humbled Himself by becoming obedient to the point of death, even death on a cross.
>
> Therefore also God highly exalted Him, and bestowed on Him the name which is above every name, that at the name of Jesus every knee should bow, of those who are in heaven, and on earth, and under the earth, and that every tongue should confess that Jesus Christ is Lord, to the glory of God the Father. (Philippians 2:1–11)

This passage ties our responsibility to humbly consider others more important than ourselves, by looking out for their interests, to the great apostle's ultimate goal of glorifying God the Father. Paul's first paragraph sets the activity of ministry within the framework of regenerated commitment to accomplishing God's purposes, and His final two paragraphs set Christ before us as the example of how this must be done. The work of Christ—His humiliation, resurrection, and exaltation—were undertaken in humble obedience, *to the glory of God the Father.* In following Christ's example, we are to be intent on one purpose—Christ's purpose, that of glorifying God the Father.

The Westminster Shorter Catechism states that "the chief end of man" is to glorify God and enjoy Him forever. In Isaiah 43, God declares that the redeemed are called by His Name and were created for His glory. If we are to fulfill the purpose for which we were created, we must not allow our dedication to the activities of interpersonal ministry to overshadow the purpose for which it was commanded. Meeting human needs must always be undertaken with the intent of glorifying God.

## Man-Centered Bible Study

When we forget the ultimate purpose behind our ministry to one another, we easily slip into the distorted practice of man-centered Bible study. I was involved for several years in a biblical counseling ministry that diligently and effectively brought the teachings of the Bible to bear on a wide variety of human needs. We unashamedly proclaimed the Bible as the infallible, inerrant Word of God that is entirely sufficient for life and godliness, and were blessed to see numerous people overcome extremely difficult problems of living by learning how to apply scriptural principles to their situations. It was an exhilarating and rewarding ministry, but it wasn't always easy.

The most difficult challenge we faced was *not* convincing people that the Bible was God's Word, or even that it was entirely sufficient to meet their needs. Our greatest challenge was keeping their focus (and ours!) on God's glory. We struggled every day to avoid presenting the Bible as a supernatural self-help technique.

We learned early on that when people are hurting, they tend to be consumed with themselves, and that we as sympathetic counselors tended to ignore that sinful self-preoccupation in our eagerness to present the "biblical answer" to all their difficulties. When we failed to deal with their fallen focus, we were actually misrepresenting God's Word as a spiritual means of meeting human-defined needs. God does not place Himself at people's disposal to help them achieve their own ends. God demands that we seek *His* kingdom and *His* righteousness, and He promises to meet all our needs as we do so (Matthew 6:33).

Our primary job as *biblical* counselors was twofold: (1) to help hurting people redefine their needs to coincide with the way God defines them in His Word, and (2) to help them allow God to meet those redefined needs according to His riches in glory so that His name could be exalted. It was a tough job, and we met with a lot of resistance. But the few who humbly submitted their needs to God's redefining process and saw Him do exceedingly abundantly above all that we ask or think made it all worthwhile.

Ministering as a biblical counselor forced me to approach Bible study from a God-centered perspective, something I might not have learned had God not providentially placed me in that position. I have since learned that it is just as easy for saints who are not necessarily struggling with overwhelming difficulties of life to approach the Bible with a self-centered agenda. We all find it easy to seek the answers *we* want in God's Word. That's why it is critically important that we consciously examine our hearts and minds each time we prepare to meet with God in His Word.

## Good Methods Are Not Enough

The very best hermeneutical[1] techniques executed with the utmost skill and creativity will not produce effective Bible study unless they are wielded by one whose heart is right with God. A receptive heart united with a teachable spirit has often made up for a lack of technique. But even the best technique cannot subdue a rebellious soul unwilling to submit to God's truth.

Paul recognizes the importance of a godly attitude when he calls upon those "who have been chosen by God, holy and beloved," to "let the peace of Christ rule in your hearts" and to "let the word of Christ richly dwell within you. . . . And whatever you do in word or deed, do all in the name of the Lord Jesus, giving thanks through Him to God the Father" (Colossians 3:12, 15–17).

Effective Bible study involves an understanding of who we are and what God requires of us. Paul tells us in this passage that we *have been chosen of God, holy and beloved.* If our faith is in Christ, we are the elect of God. He predestined us for salvation before the foundation of the world (Ephesians 1:4–6) and has seated us with Him in the heavenly places in Christ Jesus (Ephesians 2:6). Our election makes us holy and beloved in God's sight. The word "holy" refers to moral perfection and freedom from impurity.[2] God is holy because He is infinitely pure and completely untainted by evil; we are holy because we stand clothed in the righteousness of Christ, called out from the world and equipped to do His work. Because we have been chosen and set apart for holy service to a holy God, we become the specific objects of His love. He cares for us because we are His own, and He will never leave us or forsake us.

The Bible holds a unique attraction for those who are chosen of God, holy and beloved—an attraction the unregenerate cannot understand. While unsaved men and women may scorn the Bible as an irrelevant relic of antiquity, or accept it as the written record of two of the world's great religions, or even praise it as great literature, they are never drawn to it as the Word of Life from the Father of Light who wrote it to share His truth with His people.

As we prepare our hearts to meet God in His Word, we need to remind ourselves that we are *chosen, holy and beloved.* Doing that will help us study the Bible purposefully—gratefully acknowledging our undeserved standing before God and seeking His guidance to fulfill our calling.

Knowing who we are encourages us to *let the peace of Christ rule in our hearts.* Christians are at peace with God. Jesus Christ has negotiated the peace treaty, and the war is over. We are no longer God's enemies; we are now His allies. Because we are *at* peace with God, we can *have* peace in our hearts. If God is for us, who can be against us? Christians who let the peace of Christ rule in their hearts can approach Bible study confidently, knowing that "there is therefore now no condemnation for those who are in Christ Jesus" (Romans 8:1).

When we are mindful of our calling as God's holy and beloved people and are consciously allowing the peace of Christ to rule in our hearts, we are ready to approach Bible study with the intent of letting the Word of Christ richly dwell within us. The word "dwell" carries the idea of "living in" or "being at home."[3] When we are peacefully aware of who we are in God's sight, the truths of Scripture will find a comfortable home in our hearts and minds, and from that vantage point will begin to establish control over our thoughts and actions. Only by encouraging Scripture to settle in and take charge will we be able to *do all in the name of the Lord Jesus, giving thanks through Him to God the Father.*

The chosen of God should come to the Bible in humble gratitude for the gracious gift of salvation, seeking to be equipped to fulfill His purposes. Because our flesh weakens our resolve, and Satan seeks to destroy our usefulness, we must prepare our hearts and minds for study and then study intently once we are prepared.

In 2 Timothy 2:15 Paul tells us, "Be diligent to present yourself approved to God as a workman who does not need to be ashamed, handling accurately the word of truth." A Christian who comes to Bible study irreverently, selfishly, or rebelliously will not be able to handle its truths accurately and will not be able to stand before God as an unashamed worker. Before we can effectively study God's Word, we must humbly and gratefully acknowledge who we are in Him, and willingly place ourselves at His disposal to do His will.

### Good Methods Are Important

Once our hearts and minds are properly prepared to study the Bible, we must undertake that study responsibly. The Bible is sometimes difficult to understand because it was written many centuries ago by men who phrased God's truths in the context of their own cultures and lifestyles. We live in a vastly different culture today, speak a different language, and follow drastically different lifestyles. These personal and cultural factors pose some formidable interpretive challenges that can be met and overcome by the use of sound study *methods*. When we combine a properly prepared, receptive heart with reliable study skills, we can expect Bible study to bear the most nourishing and delicious fruit.

Good interpretive methods help us to accurately observe what is written in the biblical text, responsibly interpret what the written words mean, meaningfully apply what we have learned, and impact our world with our knowledge of God's truth. The remaining lessons in this study will deal with each of these areas in depth.

## Notes

1. *Hermeneutics* is the science of interpretation. R. C. Sproul explains that the word has its origin in Greek mythology. The Greek god Hermes was the messenger of the gods and his primary job was to interpret their will (R. C. Sproul, *Knowing Scripture* [Downers Grove, Ill.: InterVarsity Press, 1977], 45).

2. Charles Hodge, *Systematic Theology,* 3 vols. (Grand Rapids: Eerdmans, 1993), 1:413.

3. Spiros Zodhiates, *The Complete Word Study Dictionary* (Chattanooga: AMG Publishers, 1992), 592.

## Exercises

### Review

1. Describe a situation in which you or someone you know allowed the *activities* of ministry to overshadow the *purpose* of ministry. Did you or the person you know intend for this to happen? Why do you think it happened? How could it have been prevented?

2. How does man-centered Bible study differ from God-centered Bible study?

3. Give an example of how a well-intentioned Christian counselor might distort the Bible by presenting it as a supernatural self-help technique. How can we prevent this kind of distortion when we counsel others with Scripture?

4. Why do we usually need to redefine our "needs" when we are hurting and suffering from difficulties of living? Can you describe a time in your own life when *your* perception of your needs in a difficult situation differed from *God's* perception of your needs? How would you handle this situation if you were dealing with it now?

5. Explain why good study skills are essential to effective Bible study. Why they are not enough?

6. Explain what it means to be "chosen of God, holy and beloved."

7. Give some *specific* examples of how you can encourage the Word of God to richly dwell within you. What changes can you expect in your life if you do these things?

## *Application*

1. Read Ephesians 4–6 in your favorite Bible translation and list several verses that fall into each of the following "categories of usefulness" found in 2 Timothy 3:16–17:

   teaching (instruction):
   reproof:
   correction:
   training in righteousness:

   Now read Ephesians 4–6 in another translation and record any additional insights. How might understanding Ephesians 4–6 in the light of 2 Timothy 3:16–17 better equip you to glorify God and enjoy Him forever?

2. Read the following passage from Galatians 5:22–25:

   But the fruit of the Spirit is love, joy, peace, patience, kindness, goodness, faithfulness, gentleness, self-control; against such things there is no law. Now those who belong to Christ Jesus have crucified the flesh with its passions and desires. If we live by the Spirit, let us also walk by the Spirit.

Using a concordance and a Bible dictionary, write a definition, in your own words, for each of the following words:

love:
joy:
peace:
patience:
kindness:
goodness:
faithfulness:
gentleness:
self-control:

How does *walking by the Spirit* relate to glorifying God and enjoying Him forever?

3. Do you see any connection between the *usefulness* of Ephesians 4–6 ("Application" 1) and *walking in the Spirit?* If so, describe this relationship.

Read Ephesians 4 once more and explain what Paul means by "walking worthy of your calling."

## Digging Deeper

1. Explain how each of the following encouragements and instructions from Philippians 2:1–2 fosters a *regenerated commitment to accomplishing God's purposes,* which should surround and control the activities of ministry:

ENCOURAGEMENTS
encouragement in Christ:
consolation of love:
fellowship of the Spirit:
affection and compassion:

INSTRUCTIONS
being of the same mind:
maintaining the same love:
united in Spirit:
intent on one purpose:

Do you see any connection between the encouragements and the instructions? If so, describe them.

# LESSON 3 Seeing What Is There

*In lessons 1 and 2 we saw how important it is to understand both the unique character of the Bible and our own privileged standing before God as His chosen people. As we turn our attention to developing useful study skills, we must not lose sight of what we have already learned. Handling God's special revelation is an awesome responsibility requiring conscious submission to the illuminating work of the Holy Spirit, who takes the things of Christ and discloses them to us.*

— — —

Every effective Bible study includes three essential elements: *observation, interpretation,* and *application*. Observation answers the question, "What does it say?" Interpretation answers the question, "What does it mean?" And application answers the question, "What difference does it make?"[1]

There are many specific skills associated with observation, interpretation, and application, and you will learn some of them in the following four lessons—enough to get you started and encourage you to keep learning. You can look forward to developing many new skills of observation, interpretation, and application as you study on your own or with various groups. The recommended reading list at the end of this study contains some excellent resources to help you continue in that process.

## Begin with Observation

Effective Bible study begins with observation, progresses through interpretation, and ends with application. We can't interpret something if we don't know what it says, and we can't apply it to our lives until we know what it means. No matter how many study skills we acquire, the basic structure of effective Bible study never changes: First, *observe*, then *interpret*, finally *apply*.

This structure could be depicted graphically much like the Food Pyramid nutritionists use to help their clients develop healthy eating habits. A healthy physical diet rests on a broad base of complex carbohydrates—breads, cereals, grains, fruits, and vegetables. Add to that tasty foundation some good solid protein and a little fat, and you have a diet that will do your body good. Each element in that diet is essential to good health, but some are needed in larger quantities than others.

In much the same way, a healthy intake of Scripture rests on a broad base of observation. Add to that some good solid interpretation and a few specific, personal applications, and you are well on your way to spiritual growth. Each element in that diet is essential also, but some are needed in larger amounts than others. Just as it takes a lot of complex carbohydrates to support the specific nutritional work of protein and fat, it takes a lot of observation to support the specific spiritual work of interpretation and application.

## Observation Defined

Observation can be simply described as "paying close attention to what you see." But it's harder than most of us think. Just ask any police officer who has tried to reconstruct a traffic accident from the testimony of eyewitnesses. Not only do the people who saw the accident from different angles tell different versions of the event, but most people tend to "see" what they expect to see rather than what actually happened.

Daniel Doriani tells the story of the science professor who demonstrated this curious trait of human nature by displaying a beaker filled with horse sweat to his class of college freshmen and telling them to watch him carefully and imitate him exactly. He then dipped his index finger into the beaker and licked his finger. After each student dutifully dipped and licked his finger, the grinning professor revealed their distasteful proclivity for seeing the expected rather than the actual. "What you failed to *see,*" he said, holding up his fingers, "was that I licked my *ring* finger."[2]

We learn from these chagrined students that good observation skills don't come naturally; they must be learned. And even though basic observation skills are not difficult, they do require practice. You can't learn them by sitting in the pew and watching someone else; you have to work at them yourself.

## Look Again

Learning to be more observant requires shaking off some of those expectations that keep us from seeing what is right before us. If you want to be a more observant Bible student, you might start by laying aside (for a while) your beloved, well-worn copy of the Scriptures and picking up another translation—or several other translations. Reading those familiar verses in the phraseology of another translation, or another language if you know one, will shed a surprising amount of new light on old cherished truths. You may be amazed at how much you have missed!

A simple change of format can also be very revealing. That's why the Scripture passages quoted in this study are in paragraph form without the customary (and expected) verse designations. Even if you are familiar with the New American Standard Bible translation, you may notice in this format, words, phrases, and whole ideas that you have been reading for years *without seeing*.

## What Do You See?

Trained observers know what to look for. When Lieutenant Colombo blunders into a crime scene, he has a purpose in mind— unmasking the criminal. Years of experience (and a few good script writers) have taught him what to look for in order to accomplish his purpose. He will walk right by an obviously dead body with scarcely a glance to pick up an overlooked matchbook or a partially concealed button. He notices out-of-place furniture and missing encyclopedia volumes. He observes the scene and records those things that will help him accomplish his purpose.

When we observe a passage of Scripture, we have a purpose in mind—discovering what it means. Our task in this lesson is to learn how to look for things that will help us do that. This first stage of effective Bible study is the most time consuming *and* the most critical. Colombo would never solve a case if he failed to investigate thoroughly, and we will never discover meaning if we fail to observe just as thoroughly.

So, what kinds of things do we look for?

**Context.** Someone has said that a text without a context is a pretext. In other words, when we lift a phrase, a sentence, or a paragraph out of its literary surroundings, we can freely alter its meaning to suit our own purposes. For example, if I want to lend biblical credibility to the idea that suicide is the proper way to deal with guilt, I could use (or misuse) the following Scriptures:

> Then when Judas, who had betrayed Him, saw that He had been condemned, he felt remorse. . . . and went away and hanged himself. (Matthew 27:3, 5)

> And Jesus said . . . "Go and do the same." (Luke 10:37)

> Jesus therefore said . . . "What you do, do quickly." (John 13:27)

This line of reasoning is so blatantly distorted that most of us easily recognize and reject it; however, most context violations are far less obvious. How many Christians are aware of the context in which Jesus said, ". . . if two of you agree on earth about anything that they may ask, it shall be done for them by My Father who is in heaven. For where two or three have gathered together in My name, there I am in their midst"?[3] Most Christians are actually surprised to learn that Jesus was *not* talking about prayer in this passage, but about the process we commonly refer to as church discipline.

We miss a valuable lesson when we overlook the fact that James was discussing how we should *respond to trials* when he said, "Let everyone be quick to hear, slow to speak and slow to anger; for the anger of man does not achieve the righteousness of God" (James 1:19–20). And if we isolate Romans 8:5 from its context, we might conclude that Christians have the option of walking according to the flesh or according to the Spirit. But when we back up to verse 3 and read through verse 9, we see that Paul was teaching something very different.

Not everyone who ignores context does so with the intent to mislead or confuse. Even dedicated Bible teachers committed to teaching God's truth have been known to abuse context a little (or a lot) in their desire to make a valuable point. But good intentions don't justify irresponsible study. Second Timothy 2:15 reminds us all of our sober responsibility to handle God's Word *accurately*.

We will look at context in more detail in our next lesson, but at this point in our study we should concentrate on observing passages of Scripture in their contextual surroundings. Words derive a great deal of their meaning from the words around them. Sentences are meant to be understood in the company of their fellow sentences. Paragraphs join hands to move ideas from start to finish, and good books are built around some unifying theme. When context is ignored, the sense of the passage quickly reduces to nonsense.

***Key Words.*** Key words are those most *essential* to meaning. We know that *all* the words in a passage of Scripture are important, but some of those words bear a greater burden in transmitting the author's ideas. Our task is to discover and record those words.

We find them by looking for clues: Which words are repeated, emphasized, or used in a distinctive way? The elimination of which words would result in the loss of the author's message? Which words bring the passage to life?

When we find words that could be keys to the author's meaning, we need to highlight them in a way that focuses our attention on them. If you are artistic, get out your colored pencils and mark up the text. If you have a literary bent, rewrite those words in an eye-catching format or style. You engineering and accounting types might even want to display them on a chart. The important thing here is flagging words you think are *key* so that you can find them again when you need them. How you do that is up to you.

Remember that key words are not always impressive words. Neither are key words always single words; sometimes they are phrases. Frequently the little word *but* unlocks the meaning of a passage, and a phrase like "and they will know that I am the Lord their God" points directly to the author's purpose for writing.

**Lists.** Identify and mark any lists you find in the passage. There are some good examples of lists in Romans 1 and Galatians 5. See if you can find them. Lists are important to meaning because they contain items that have something in common. Determining what they have in common is a clue to the passage's meaning. Mark these lists in any way that helps you see them clearly. If you find more than one list in a passage, see if they relate to each other in some way. (Two of the lists in Galatians 5 definitely relate to each other. Do you see how?)

**Comparisons and Contrasts.** A tremendous amount of meaning can be conveyed through the use of comparison and contrast. Your best clues for discovering comparisons and contrasts are words such as "like," "as," "but," and "however." Some comparisons and contrasts are not so clearly marked, but you will begin to see them as your skills of observation improve.

Comparisons and contrasts convey meaning powerfully, but sometimes they send you scurrying for additional information. For example, in Philippians 2:17 and 2 Timothy 4:6, Paul compares himself to a drink offering. If you have no idea what a drink offering is, you will have to find out before you understand what he means.

**Presentation of Ideas.** Much of the Bible communicates *concepts* or *ideas* rather than facts or historical events. Therefore, it is very helpful to begin recognizing the different ways concepts or ideas can be presented. Some writers use a series of simple statements to build a complicated concept, while others start with the complicated concept and break it down into its simpler elements. Some writers present concepts by describing actions and their consequences, and some use a process of clarification or explanation to communicate concepts. Don't get discouraged if you have trouble recognizing these; it gets easier with practice. At this point, be alert to "building" and "separating" words like *and, but, if, then, since, whenever, however, in addition to,* and *now that.* Also, pay attention to summaries, restatements, and illustrations.

***Journalism Questions.*** Journalists are excellent investigators, and they build their investigations around six questions: Who? What? When? Where? How? and Why? We can unearth a lot of clues to meaning in a biblical passage by following their example. *Who* is the author and *who* is his intended audience? *Who* are the primary actors in a passage? *What* events or actions are taking place, and *what* words are spoken? *When* does the author write? *Where* is he and *where* is his recipient? *How* does he get his message across? *How* does he expect his readers to respond? *Why* does he write? *Why* do his readers need to hear what he has to say?

When you are observing a passage with these journalism questions, be very careful to respond with answers you actually see in the text. It is very easy to get carried away with speculation, particularly when you are asking "Why?" questions.

***Questions for Further Research and Study.*** During the observation process, you will come across many things that you don't understand or that alert you to a need for further research. Paul's comparison of himself to a drink offering in Philippians and 2 Timothy is a good example. If you have never heard of a drink offering before, record this question ("What is a drink offering?") and the reference that stimulated it (Philippians 2:17; 2 Timothy 4:6), and go on with your observations. Sometimes further observation will answer a question before you go charging down a rabbit trail and lose your concentration on the task at hand.

***Outlining and Titling.*** If you are observing a long passage or one that is complicated, your final observation activity should be trying to outline it or break it into sections with titles. This is more difficult for some people than for others, but most students actually learn to enjoy it after some practice. Outlining or titling helps you organize the passage so that you can easily remember its key points.

### Let It Soak Awhile

When you have completed your observation of a passage, lay it aside and let it soak into your mind for a while before you plunge into interpretation. Do something totally unrelated for several hours or an entire day. If you have done your observations well, you will probably find your thoughts returning to the passage frequently during your time away. If you get any brilliant insights, jot them down, but don't rush back to your study too soon. Give the Holy Spirit time to work into you what you have worked out of the passage.

## Notes

1. For an in-depth analysis of these three elements, see Howard G. Hendricks and William D. Hendricks, *Living by the Book* (Chicago: Moody Press, 1991).

2. Adapted from Daniel M. Doriani, *Getting the Message: A Plan for Interpreting and Applying the Bible* (Phillipsburg, N.J.: P&R Publishing, 1996), 14.

3. Matthew 18:19–20.

## Exercises

### Review

1. Briefly define observation, interpretation, and application and explain how they relate to each other.

2. Why are good skills of observation important to effective Bible study? What kinds of things hinder our ability to observe accurately?

3. Explain the following statement in your own words: "A text without a context is a pretext." What does this statement have to do with Bible study?

4. What are "key words," and how do they contribute to effective Bible study?

5. List at least five things you need to look for when you are observing a passage of Scripture, and explain how each might help you understand the author's meaning.

6. Do you agree that it is a good idea to let your observations of Scripture "soak in" for a while before you begin to interpret a passage? Why or why not?

## *Application*

1. To practice the skills you have learned in this lesson, observe Ephesians 4:1–7, 4:17–5:2, 5:15–6:9, 6:18–20, and Colossians 3:1–4:6 as thoroughly as you can. (These passages are reproduced in appendix A.) Fill out the following chart on a separate page.

| OBSERVATION | EPHESIANS | COLOSSIANS |
| --- | --- | --- |
| key words: | | |
| comparisons and contrasts: | | |
| lists: | | |
| relationship between ideas: | | |
| journalism questions:<br>  *Who?*<br>  *What?*<br>  *When?*<br>  *Where?* | | |

| OBSERVATION | EPHESIANS | COLOSSIANS |
|---|---|---|
| journalism questions: (continued) *How?* *Why?* | | |
| questions for future study and research: | | |

2. Now, try to outline or title each passage:

3. Based solely on your observation of these passages, answer the following questions: How does Paul describe a worthy walk? How are a person's attitudes, thoughts, and actions involved in a worthy walk? Why does Paul believe it is important for Christians to keep seeking the things above? How does he say we can do that? How does *being filled with the Spirit* relate to *letting the Word of Christ richly dwell within you?* (Hint: List the consequences [or results] of being filled with the Spirit and letting the Word of Christ richly dwell within you, and note any similarities.)

4. Observe Matthew 22:34–40 and answer the following question: Did Jesus command us to love ourselves? Explain your answer based *solely* on your observations of the passage.

### Digging Deeper

1. Observe Luke 24:13–35. Based *solely* on your observations of this passage, are you more inclined to think that these two disciples were (1) Cleopas and another man, or (2) Cleopas and his wife?

   Obviously, the passage does not tell us who the other disciple was, but take a position and support it *solely* from your observations. Then take the other position and support it solely from your observations of the passage.

Do some research and find out all you can about Cleopas's wife. Does your research move you toward one position or the other? Explain.

# 4

## Crossing Bridges to Meaning

*Most of us are understandably intimidated by the very idea of interpreting the Bible. Seeking to declare the meaning of God's holy Word is a sober task that calls us to serious-minded effort. As responsible students of the Bible, we must never underestimate our obligation to handle the Word of Truth accurately. But we must also remember that God wrote the Book to reveal His truth to us, not to hide it—and for that reason, our obligation to understand it is at least as great as our obligation to revere it.*

John Calvin said, ". . . the first business of an interpreter [is] to let his author say what he does say, instead of attributing to him what we think he ought to say."[1] Calvin, who has been called the greatest exegete of the Reformation, understood the connection between good observation and good interpretation. Responsible interpretation begins and ends with observation. We interpret what we have observed and then check back to make sure our interpretations are entirely consistent with those observations.

### Look for a Bridge
Right now as you stand on the solid ground of your observations and look across the yawning gulf that separates you from the

meaning of those observations, you may be wondering how in the world you are ever going to get across. Well, don't even think about jumping. Look for a bridge.

One of the most secure bridges from observation to meaning is the *Bridge of Purpose and Themes*. Look through your stockpile of observations to find clues that point you to the author's purpose for writing. Some writers make this amazingly easy. The beloved apostle John leaves no doubt in our minds about his purposes for writing his books and letters:

> These [things] have been written that you may believe that Jesus is the Christ, the Son of God; and that believing you may have life in His name. (John 20:31)

> These things I have written to you who believe in the name of the Son of God, in order that you may know that you have eternal life. (1 John 5:13)

> I was in the Spirit on the Lord's day, and I heard behind me a loud voice like the sound of a trumpet, saying, "Write in a book what you see, and send it to the seven churches: to Ephesus and to Smyrna and to Pergamum and to Thyatira and to Sardis and to Philadephia and to Laodicea." (Revelation 1:10–11)

The little epistle of Jude also contains a crystal-clear purpose statement:

> Beloved, while I was making every effort to write you about our common salvation, I felt the necessity to write to you appealing that you contend earnestly for the faith which was once for all delivered to the saints. (v. 3)

And Luke tells us right up front why he is writing a life of Christ:

> Inasmuch as many have undertaken to compile an account of the things accomplished among us, just as those who from the beginning were eyewitnesses and servants of the

word have handed them down to us, it seemed fitting for
me as well, having investigated everything carefully from
the beginning, to write it out for you in consecutive order,
most excellent Theophilus. (Luke 1:1–3)

Not all biblical authors state their purposes for writing so straight-
forwardly, but they all *did have* a purpose for writing. And they all
left clues to help us find it. Who is the author and to whom is he
writing? Does he give any indication of the circumstances that
prompted him to write to these particular people? What is his attitude toward them? Does he mention any specific needs that
might have prompted him to write?

Go over the key words and phrases you identified. What did the
author talk about most? What kind of language does he use? What
subjects does he keep coming back to? Does he spend most of his
time communicating ideas, discussing behavior, or chronicling
historical events?

Look over your questions for further research to see if the answers to any of them might help you locate the author's purpose.
For example, if you don't know why the Philippians were being
persecuted or who was distorting the gospel in Galatia, do a little
research in a Bible encyclopedia to find out. Answers to those kinds
of questions can bring a fuzzy speculation about the author's purpose into sharp focus.

If you have done your observations thoroughly, they will lead
you to the author's purpose for writing. Once you have found it,
write a concise statement of it in your own words, and *use it* as a
bridge to interpretation. The author will write to accomplish his
purpose. If you are coming up with interpretations that don't fit
his purpose for writing, either you are off track in your interpretations or you have misunderstood his purpose.

If you are studying a short passage of Scripture, take the time
to examine the book in which it occurs to find the author's purpose for writing. Jesus' Sermon on the Mount and Upper Room
Discourse can be easily distorted if they are interpreted without
reference to Matthew's and John's purposes for writing their
gospels.

Let your *purpose statement* help you identify major *themes* in the author's book. The author's purpose tells you *why* he is writing; his themes describe *how* he accomplishes his purpose. For example, Paul wrote his second letter to Timothy to instruct and encourage him as he prepared to assume the role of leadership in the church.

The letter contains several themes that support Paul's purpose: Paul's instructions and encouragement center on (1) Timothy's responsibilities toward the treasure of the gospel, (2) his willingness to face suffering, (3) his personal example as a leader, and (4) his ministry activities. A good way to determine whether you have identified all the major themes in a book is to see if you can outline the book using each theme as a major heading. If you have a lot of material that doesn't fit anywhere, you may be missing a theme or two.

Don't allow yourself to get frustrated if your best study buddy comes up with a set of themes that differs from yours in number or focus. The themes I have identified for 2 Timothy above are very broad, and each will encompass a great deal of material in Paul's book. A good friend of mine came up with several additional themes, but hers were much more specific. When we compared notes, we discovered that we had unearthed the same basic truths even though we had chosen to present them differently. I prefer to present truths in broad strokes, while she usually opts for finer detail. Our differing styles reflect accurate and responsible interpretations of Paul's letter to Timothy couched in terms that reflect our individual personalities.

### Another Bridge

Another helpful bridge from observation to interpretation is the *Bridge of Ever-Widening Context*. Since you have already observed the *immediate* context of the passage of Scripture you are studying, you can bridge the gap to interpretation by remembering that God wrote the *whole* Bible with a specific purpose in mind. Even though God used many human authors to record His message over a period of several centuries, the resulting Book consistently reflects His purpose in writing. God does not contradict Himself in

His Book, and our confidence in His sovereignty enables us responsibly to let Scripture interpret Scripture.[2]

Whenever we encounter a passage that can reasonably be interpreted in two or more ways, we must accept the interpretation that is consistent with the entire message of the Bible. By way of example, see if you can detect two legitimate interpretations of the following sentence: "Grandma loves climbing grapevines." With no context to guide you, you have no idea whether Grandma is doing the climbing or the grapevines are! Common sense would lead you to assume that the grapevines are climbing and Grandma is loving them—unless the sentence occurs in a story about "Grandma," Little Timmy's pet lizard.

My husband, Frank, once had an employee who was a wonderful person but a not-so-great worker. When the man told him he had found another job and asked my husband to write a reference for him, Frank was a bit frustrated. He didn't want to hurt the fellow's chances of getting the job, but neither did he want to lie about his work record. After struggling for several days, he finally wrote the following reference: "If you can get this man to work for you, you will really be fortunate."

We can be thankful that God doesn't communicate with us ambiguously. He *wants* us to understand what He says, and He gives us all the information we need in His Word. Accurately understanding God's message requires us to interpret particular passages of Scripture within the ever-widening context of the "full counsel of God," and the ability to do that doesn't come overnight.

I'm sure we all know experienced Bible teachers who seem to have all the relevant passages right at their fingertips, and most of us have despaired of ever being able to emulate them. Such thorough knowledge of the Bible reflects years of intense study that the typical Christian cannot reasonably undertake, but that does not mean we must abandon hope of ever being able to interpret the Bible accurately. Bible scholars down through the ages have left us numerous helps to assist us as we seek to let Scripture interpret Scripture.

A good place to start is with the cross references in your own Bible. Many of these references will lead you to other verses that deal with words or topics addressed in the passage you are studying. Some study Bibles use a system of chain references or color coding that will actually lead you through a study of a particular topic. An exhaustive concordance will give you every verse in the Bible where a particular word is used, and a topical Bible like *Nave's* will give you verses related to a particular subject. Resources like these are well worth the investment.

As you continue to study, you will become more familiar with the Bible as a whole and will find yourself remembering related passages on your own. This is why establishing some kind of systematic reading program is so important to responsible Bible study. There are many excellent reading plans to choose from. The one you choose is not nearly as important as your *faithful use* of the one you choose. As you read, jot notes in the margin of your Bible regarding words or topics covered in that passage or start a card file referencing verses dealing with particular subjects. Either system will help you locate relevant passages when you need them for a later study.

Remember also that commentaries can be an invaluable aid to responsible interpretation when they are used correctly. Do your own study first; then read several commentaries to see how other students of the Word have interpreted the passage you are studying. You can learn a great deal from the experience and perspective of those who have been studying and teaching the Scriptures for many years.

## Scenic Bridges

The *Bridge of Purposes and Themes* and the *Bridge of Ever-Widening Context* lead directly from your observations to interpretation. But there are a couple of other bridges spanning that chasm that take a more circuitous route through some delightfully scenic territory.

The first is the *Bridge of Historical Background*. The Bible was written many centuries ago in times very different from our own. Before we can interpret the Bible responsibly, we need to learn a little about the historical and cultural setting in which it was written. The parable of the Good Samaritan loses a good deal of its punch if we fail to unearth the first-century Jewish attitudes toward Samaritans, and the book of Ruth takes on a whole new meaning when we take the time to learn about the Moabites. Bible encyclopedias, commentaries, and books dealing with biblical customs are excellent sources of historical insight and should not be neglected in your study.

Another scenic route crosses over the *Bridge of Grammatical Structure.* The Bible was written in words, phrases, sentences, and paragraphs, and is not exempt from the rules of grammar that structure any type of effective writing. Nouns are nouns, verbs are verbs, and modifiers are modifiers. Understanding the relationship between the basic parts of a sentence is essential to interpretation. If we can't identify *who said what to whom* or *who did what to another,* we won't have a clue as to what is going on.

If history and grammar were not your favorite subjects in school, don't despair. Remember you are using them as bridges to responsible biblical interpretation, and that should enhance your interest in them considerably. A friend of mine grew up speaking English as a second language and never could get the hang of English grammar until he went to seminary and had to learn it to understand Greek. His desire to study the Bible effectively was all the motivation he needed to master what had previously been impossible for him. Today he diagrams English sentences better than most English teachers I know! If you need a refresher course in ancient history or English grammar, don't hesitate to jump in with enthusiasm. The Holy Spirit will bless your efforts exceedingly abundantly above all you can ask or think.

# Notes

1. Quoted in Louis Berkhof, *Principles of Biblical Interpretation* (Grand Rapids: Baker, 1950), 27.

2. In theological circles this principle of interpretation is called "the analogy of faith." See R. C. Sproul, *Knowing Scripture* (Downers Grove, Ill.: InterVarsity Press, 1977) for a more detailed discussion of this principle.

# *Exercises*

## *Review*

1. Explain in your own words the quotation from John Calvin at the outset of this lesson. How does this quotation demonstrate his understanding of the connection between observation and interpretation?

2. Explain how each of the four bridges discussed in this lesson will help you cross the "yawning gulf" between observation and interpretation.

    Bridge of Purposes and Themes:
    Bridge of Ever-Widening Context:
    Bridge of Historical Background:
    Bridge of Grammatical Structure:

3. Distinguish between purpose and themes.

4. What are some ways you can begin to let *Scripture interpret Scripture* even if you have only been studying the Bible for a short while?

5. Explain why an understanding of history and grammatical structure is important to responsible interpretation of the Bible.

## *Application*

1. Rewrite the purpose statements contained in the following verses in your own words: (Hint: How would you explain the purpose of each of these books to someone if you didn't have your Bible with you and hadn't memorized these verses? Begin by saying, "John [or Jude, or Luke] wrote this book in order to . . . ")

    John 20:31:
    1 John 5:13:
    Revelation 1:10–11:

Jude 3:
Luke 1:1–3:

2. Set aside an hour to read carefully through the books of Ephesians and Colossians to see if you can detect Paul's *purpose* for writing these books.
   Can you find a specific purpose statement in either book? If so, record it. If not, state Paul's purposes in your own words and explain how you arrived at them.
   Did your observations of parts of Ephesians and Colossians in lesson 3 help you determine Paul's purposes? If so, how?
   See if you can detect any of Paul's *themes* that help him accomplish his purposes for writing these books.

3. Begin a systematic reading program that will take you through the entire Bible in a year or less. Become accountable to a friend or relative who will help you remain faithful to your commitment.

## Digging Deeper

1. Do some historical research in a Bible encyclopedia, a book on Bible customs, and relevant commentaries to find out all you can about the Colossians and the Ephesians at the time Paul wrote to them. How does your historical understanding of the letters enhance your ability to interpret what Paul is saying in the portions of these books we have been examining in this study?

2. Examine the grammatical structure of the following sentence: "These things I have written to you who believe in the name of the Son of God, in order that you may know that you have eternal life."

   nouns:
   verbs:
   modifiers (adjectives and adverbs):
   prepositions:

conjunctions:
leftovers:
independent clause(s):
dependent clause(s):
main subject of the sentence:
main verb of the sentence:
diagram or structure of the sentence:

How has this grammar exercise helped you understand this sentence?

# 5

# Making Sense of Literature

*Few Christians appreciate the magnificent privilege of owning a Bible. Most of us own several, and we may have based our purchasing decisions on something as frivolous as the color of the cover. We carry them to church, stick them in our purses, and toss them into the glove compartment of the car. We open them when we're instructed, read them when we're reminded, and forget them when we're busy. We don't mean to be disrespectful; we just don't realize the extent of our blessings. Most of us are blissfully unaware of the awesome price our ancestors paid to give us a Bible written in our own language—and the freedom to interpret it privately. Because we undervalue our privileges, we also underestimate our responsibilities. How easily we forget that to whom much has been given, much is required.*

Biblically illiterate Christians are woefully ill-equipped to be effective disciples. When Jesus calls us to follow Him, He expects us to *follow* Him, and we can only do that by keeping Him in sight. Our sole means of "seeing" Jesus today is by studying His Word under the illuminating power of the Holy Spirit. The Bible contains our marching orders, and we can't move obediently until we understand them.

If we are to be effective disciples, we must do more than carry the Book or read the Book or recommend the Book. We must obey the Book—and obedience requires understanding. We can't apply what we don't understand. Understanding begins with observation and is facilitated by the bridges that lead from facts to meaning. Once across those bridges, we can begin to interpret the text by adhering to some basic study techniques that have successfully guided those who have faithfully followed our Lord throughout the centuries.

## Literal Sense Versus Literal Nonsense

Have you ever told someone you take the Bible literally only to have her come back with something like, "Oh, so you believe God has feathers?" Comments like that usually reflect a contentious spirit, but they may also reveal a basic misunderstanding of *literal interpretation*. When we say we interpret a piece of writing *literally,* we mean that we pay close attention to the meaning of the words used in the literary context in which they are found. For example, look at the common phrase in the following sentences:

> I have gained so much weight that most of my clothes are *coming apart at the seams.*

> My husband has been under so much stress at work that he is *coming apart at the seams.*

You can easily see how that phrase conveys meaning in both sentences even though we would not interpret it *literally* the same way in both cases. My clothes have literal seams that are actually coming apart under the strain of my additional weight; my husband does not (unless he has recently undergone a surgical procedure). So, how do we know that the second sentence speaks of my husband's mental and emotional state? Because we interpret the sentence with *literal sense* rather than *literal nonsense*.

Interpreting with literal sense requires us to determine the precise meanings of the words used by an author and to evaluate them in the setting in which they are found. A sentence like "This heart has been torn apart" contains simple, easy-to-define words, but standing alone, it can be difficult to interpret. It would mean one thing coming from the pen of a jilted lover and something quite different coming from the mouth of a trauma surgeon. We need to remember that the Bible is *literature*. Responsibly interpreting God's revelation requires us to seek its meaning in *literary* terms. The first step in that process is determining what kind of literature we are reading. Language, even when used to describe the same event, varies depending on the purpose for which it is employed. The newspaper account of a tragic accident would hardly resemble the eulogy given at the funeral of one of the victims.

## Literary Devices

Before we seek to interpret a passage of Scripture, we must determine whether it is part of a letter, a poem, a historical account, a parable, or a predictive prophecy. Given the setting of the passage, we also need to look for various literary devices used by authors to transmit specific meaning to their readers.

**Hyperbole** is exaggeration used to make a point. Note the rather obvious differences in the following two sentences:

> The much-anticipated game between the Brigham Young University Cougars and the University of New Mexico Lobos drew a crowd of 46,783 people to University Stadium Saturday night.

> The whole city of Albuquerque crammed into University Stadium Saturday night to watch their Lobos make mincemeat out of the BYU Cougars.

Both sentences provide some basic facts about the game. However, the second uses hyperbole to transmit some additional information (like whom the writer was pulling for!)

**Personification** is a poetic device that attributes human characteristics to inanimate objects or animals. When we read in Scripture about rocks breaking forth into singing and trees clapping their hands, we immediately recognize personification. Giving God physical attributes such as eyes, ears, arms, or wings is another form of personification found in the Bible.

Responsible biblical interpretation requires us to distinguish carefully between personification and historical narrative. The *meaning* of the scriptural passages dealing with Balaam's eloquent donkey and Jonah's fishy accommodations can be severely distorted if we read personification into passages intended as historical accounts.

**Metaphors** are figures of speech in which words or phrases are used in creative ways to signify analogies or likenesses. When Jesus says, "I am the door," we don't expect to find a door knob in the center of His chest. We understand that He is comparing Himself to an entryway of some kind.

**Similes** establish direct comparisons through the use of the words *like* and *as*. When Paul tells us he is being "poured out like a drink offering," he is using a simile to compare his life of ministry to one of the Old Testament offerings.[1]

The literary character of the Bible also requires us to pay particular attention to the meanings of the words we encounter in our text. Many times we read right over a word, thinking we know what it means, only to be stopped dead in our tracks when someone asks us for a definition. The words you have identified as key to the passage are especially important; make sure you know what they mean.

Some words have more than one meaning and should be evaluated carefully to determine which meaning is appropriate to the passage you are studying. "God's will," for example, can mean (1) God's precepts revealed for His people, (2) God's sovereign action by which He brings to pass whatever happens, or (3) that which is pleasing to God.[2] The meaning we read into a verse like 2 Peter 3:9 must be carefully determined by context and by the whole counsel of God if we are to interpret the passage responsibly.

### *Implicit by Explicit, Unclear by Clear*
Implications drawn from Scripture should always be supported by clearly stated teaching. Since it is very easy to jump to conclusions

(or, in this case, to implications), we must exercise great care to interpret only on the basis of what we have clearly observed in the text. For example, how many times have you heard someone teach that angels are genderless, on the basis of Mark 12:25? Take a look. The passage doesn't say that.

Difficult passages of Scripture should be interpreted in light of what is clearly understandable. For example, Hebrews 6:4–6 and 10:27–28 cannot be interpreted responsibly unless they are studied in conjunction with passages like John 10 and Romans 8.

## Special Forms of Literature

Some of the literature we encounter in Scripture requires special handling to ensure accurate interpretation.

**Historical narrative,** as innocuous as it may seem, can trip us up if we fail to interpret it correctly. Historical narrative describes the world events and human activities involved in God's work of revealing His truth to His people. But the *interpretation* of those events is left to the didactic (teaching or instructing) portions of Scripture.

For example, the Gospels, which are largely historical narrative, record the events and activities surrounding the establishment of the Lord's Supper, while the apostle Paul in his *didactic* epistles teaches us the significance of that sacrament.

We need to be careful about drawing inferences and basing doctrine solely on historical narrative. The historical account of David's life in the Old Testament does not allow us to infer that his sins were acceptable behavior for a "man after God's own heart." In a similar way, we cannot overthrow the doctrine of the omniscience of God based on the historical account of God's seeking Adam and Eve in the Garden after they had sinned.

Of course, the most important interpretative skill regarding historical narrative is the simple ability to recognize it. Failure to identify biblical accounts of events—such as Creation, the destruction of Sodom and Gomorrah, and Elijah and Elisha's miraculous activities—as historical narrative rather than allegory always results in serious misinterpretation.

**Parables** are illustrative stories used by Jesus to reveal the mysteries of the kingdom to His disciples while concealing them from His enemies. When parables are confused with allegories, they are usually interpreted wrongly. Allegories are complex illustrative stories in which every detail carries some kind of comparative significance while parables are simpler stories intended to teach one specific point. When we study a parable we need to concentrate on the basic point of the story without trying to draw meaning from every detail.

In Jesus' Parable of the Sower, He describes seed that has been sown on four different types of soil—only one of which produces growth. In explaining this parable to His disciples, Jesus specifically identifies the sower as the Son of Man, the seed as the gospel, and the different kinds of soil as those who hear the gospel.

The point of the parable is that reception of the gospel depends on the type of heart upon which it falls. Just as seed will not germinate in the wrong kind of soil, the gospel will not take root in a heart that has not been prepared by God to receive it. We must be careful, however, not to read more into the parable than Jesus intended. Even though some soils "naturally" support growth, we cannot conclude that some hearts will respond without divine preparation. Scripture teaches elsewhere that no fallen human being responds "naturally" to the Word.

**Proverbs** are short pithy statements filled with wisdom for godly living. They should not be confused with moral absolutes. "Train up a child in the way he should go, and when he is old he will not depart from it" (Prov. 22:6 NKJV) is not an ironclad promise that all children raised according to biblical principles will become godly adults, but a truism that is generally applicable to humanity as a whole.

**Hebrew poetry** usually consists of two lines, the second of which looks back at the first and restates it, expands it, intensifies it, or comments on it. We find most of the Hebrew poetry in the Bible in the Old Testament, but some has been carried over into the New Testament as well. Understanding its parallel structure helps us interpret it correctly.

**Predictive prophecy** is the most difficult type of biblical literature to interpret properly. Responsible Bible students are particularly careful to let Scripture interpret Scripture when dealing with predictive prophecy and recognize the pitfalls of venturing outside the pages of Scripture in search of prophetic fulfillment. The apocalyptic literature found in Daniel, Ezekiel, and Revelation contains much unexplained symbolic imagery that requires special handling beyond the scope of this study. Students who are interested in studying this type of literature should consult with their pastor or elders for guidance.

## *Interpret Responsibly*
Responsible biblical interpretation encompasses more than the techniques we employ in studying the words written on the pages of God's holy Word. It also requires a heart attuned to God's purposes and willing to obey what it understands. Study that stops short of application produces fools, not followers. Before we move on to lesson 6, spend some time alone with your Father and reaffirm your commitment to put the things you have learned into practice in your daily life.

# Notes

1. Our discussion of literary analysis in this short study is necessarily limited. Students who wish to know more about this fascinating subject are referred to Louis Berkhof's more detailed discussion in chapter 5 of *Principles of Biblical Interpretation* (Grand Rapids: Baker, 1950).

2. R. C. Sproul, *Knowing Scripture* (Downers Grove, Ill.: InterVarsity Press, 1977), 81.

# Exercises

## *Review*
1. What part does Bible study play in discipleship?

2. Explain, in your own words, the difference between interpreting with *literal sense* and with *literal nonsense*. Give some examples from your own experience if you can.

3. Why is it important to know whether a passage of Scripture is part of a letter or a historical account?

4. Define each of the following literary devices and give an example of each:

   hyperbole:
   personification:
   metaphor:
   simile:

5. What is the difference between an allegory and a parable? What kind of interpretive problems result from treating a parable like an allegory?

## Application

1. Spend some time examining your Bible and list all the different types of literature you find there.

2. Describe in your own words what Jesus is teaching about Himself when He uses each of the following metaphors. (Hint: Pay particular attention to the context of each statement. What is going on around Jesus when He makes each of these statements? How does the context help you understand what He means by what He says?)

   "I am the bread of life." (John 6:35, 48):
   "I am the light of the world." (John 9:5):
   "I am the door." (John 10:9):
   "I am the good shepherd." (John 10:11, 14):
   "I am the resurrection and the life." (John 11:25):
   "I am the way, and the truth, and the life." (John 14:6):
   "I am the vine, and you are the branches." (John 15:5):

3. Go through the passages from Ephesians and Colossians printed in appendix A and note any literary devices Paul uses to communicate with his readers. How do these *devices* enhance your understanding of the passages? What *type* of literature are these passages from Ephesians and Colossians? How might that affect your understanding of Paul's message?

## *Digging Deeper*

1. Does John 3:15 negate the Reformed teachings of election and predestination? Study this verse in the light of John 6, particularly verse 37, and other applicable Scriptures before you answer. Explain your reasoning fully.

2. Read the accounts of Balaam and Jonah in Numbers 22 and Jonah 1–4. How would you defend the descriptions of the eloquent donkey and Jonah's fishy accommodations as historical narrative rather than personification?

3. What does Mark 12:25 teach about angels? Consult a concordance and do some research on angels. Based on your research, do you believe angels are genderless? Why or why not?

4. Rewrite the account of either Jonah or Philemon (found in the books bearing their names) as newspaper articles. You may choose whether you want your article to appear on the first page of the early edition as a news item or in the Sunday morning feature section as a human interest article. If you have time, try rewriting the other account as a poem or a short story.

# LESSON 6
# Making Changes in Our Lives

*The world is full of people who know a great deal about the Bible.
You can find them on college campuses, behind church pulpits,
and working in offices. You can read their books, listen to them
on the radio, and discuss their ideas for days on end. You may
be so impressed by the breadth and depth of their scriptural
knowledge that you completely overlook the acid test of spiritual wisdom: Do they apply what they have learned? What difference has their learning made in their lives? Are they fools or
followers?*

A s we move into the application stage of our study, we will find
ourselves shifting gears rather dramatically. Up to this point, we
have tried to remain as objective as possible in order to protect
our study from the danger of what scholars call "subjectivism." Subjectivism is looking at a passage of Scripture and saying, "My interpretation is just as valid as yours even though they disagree.
There is no objective truth in Scripture. What I see there is true for
me, and what you see there is true for you."

Subjectivism undercuts the very idea of revealed truth because
it makes the *reader* the determiner of meaning rather than the *author*. It reduces Bible study to little more than a creative mental

jaunt through an elusive fantasy land. The observation and interpretation stage of effective Bible study must be conscientiously guarded against our personal biases if we are to allow the author to say what he says instead of what we want him to say.

However, once we have objectively allowed the author to speak, we must expose ourselves to his message, and we can only do that *subjectively*. *Subjectivity* is not the same thing as *subjectivism*. Subjectivity recognizes that if you and I disagree on our interpretation of a passage, then at least one of us is wrong. We cannot both be right. Subjectivity demands a meeting of our minds in the area of interpretation but expects us to part company as we apply that interpretation. Responsible biblical interpretation requires us to converge around the author's meaning while meaningful biblical application requires us to diverge in our own individual employment of that meaning.

## Applying the Principle

The distinction between subjectivism and subjectivity is often blurred when we confuse the *principles* taught in a passage of Scripture with the countless possible *applications* of those principles. For example, let's look at one particular principle from Titus 2:3–5 that all young Christian women should apply, but not necessarily in the same way.

> Older women likewise are to be reverent in their behavior, not malicious gossips, not enslaved to much wine, teaching what is good, that they may encourage the young women to love their husbands, to love their children, to be sensible, pure, workers at home, kind, being subject to their own husbands, that the word of God may not be dishonored.

The phrase "workers at home" in this passage has generated a great deal of dissension in the church of Jesus Christ because of a failure to distinguish the principle from the application. The *principle* Paul is teaching in this passage is that a young Christian woman should place a high priority on her responsibilities to her family; the *application* encompasses the myriad of ways she could do that.

Making the family a high priority *includes* working at home, but it does not necessarily exclude working outside the home. Some women cannot hold down a job and fulfill their biblical responsibilities to their families. Others cannot fulfill those responsibilities without that job. In some cases the outside job reflects a heart of greedy self-centeredness. In other cases it mirrors selfless, sacrificial love. Individual family situations determine how a young woman must fulfill her biblical responsibilities to her own family.

Confusing application with principle fosters arrogant attitudes in the body of Christ, which breed disharmony and dissension. A woman I know has disrupted at least four churches because of her attitude on this very issue. In her mind, any married woman who works outside of her home is sinning and in need of discipline. Unfortunately, she takes it upon herself to do the disciplining. Several groups of church elders have attempted to correct her thinking in this area, but she has stubbornly refused to budge.

As we learn to apply scriptural truth in our lives, we must guard against confusing principles with applications. We all operate with the same principles, but their applications to our different lives and circumstances may vary widely. Expecting uniformity in our interpretation of principles is biblically responsible, but demanding uniformity in our application of those principles is destructive.

## Believing in God

R. C. Sproul has said that the real issue of faith is not so much whether we believe *in* God, but whether we believe the God we believe in.[1] If we believe the God we believe in, we will not only study His Word, but also change. Our *thinking* will change, our *attitudes* will change, and our *behavior* will change.

Effective application of biblical truth involves three areas. Typically it begins with our thoughts, moves on to our attitudes, and ultimately impacts our behavior. A young friend of mine used to say that your body won't go where your mind hasn't already been. He was right.

Scriptural application that pleases God does more than conform our behavior to some legalistic standard. It also aligns our thinking with His will and develops attitudes consistent with His nature.

As we concentrate on developing the mind of Christ within us as regenerated beings, we will find *lasting behavioral change* much easier to accomplish.

## The Battle for Your Mind

The apostle Paul understood the necessity of bringing our minds under the control of the Holy Spirit if we are to walk in a manner worthy of our calling in this fallen world. In 2 Corinthians 10:3–5 he tells us, "Though we walk in the flesh, we do not war according to the flesh, for the weapons of our warfare are not of the flesh, but divinely powerful for the destruction of fortresses. We are destroying speculations and every lofty thing raised up against the knowledge of God, and we are taking every thought captive to the obedience of Christ." Because our redeemed natures live in a house of fallen flesh, we are constantly being assaulted by temptations to live unrighteously, and the Enemy's battle plan calls for occupation of our minds.

Paul describes our defensive battle plan for taking every thought captive to the obedience of Christ in Philippians 4:8: "Finally, brethren, whatever is true, whatever is honorable, whatever is right, whatever is pure, whatever is lovely, whatever is of good repute, if there is any excellence and if anything worthy of praise, let your mind dwell on these things."

In the battle for your mind, the Enemy desires to infiltrate your thinking with unrighteous ideas. Defending against his schemes requires you to identify those unrighteous ideas and refuse them entrance to your mind. You can do that in a figurative sense by throwing all approaching thoughts up against the wall and frisking them with Philippians 4:8. If you find any of the Enemy's deceitful weapons concealed in those thoughts, disarm them before you allow them to dwell in your mind.

## Attitude Adjustments

As we develop and practice habits of godly thinking, we will find our *attitudes* changing as well. An attitude can be described as a specific mental perspective that colors the way we look at life and determines the quality of our obedience. We've all heard the story of the mutinous five year old who, after being forced to sit down by his out-of-patience mother, cried out indignantly, "I may be sitting on the outside, but I'm standing up on the inside." He had been forced into compliance with his mother's wishes, but the *quality* of his obedience was tainted with rebellion because his attitude was wrong.

The New Testament tells us that God-honoring attitudes consist of three essential qualities. First, they are *righteous*. Luke 1:17 says that John the Baptist came in the spirit and power of Elijah "to turn the hearts of the fathers back to the children, and the disobedient to the attitude of righteousness; so as to make ready a people prepared for the Lord." Filling our minds with righteous thoughts paints our view of life with righteous hues and generates godly motives for our behavior. We learn to look at the circumstances of our lives from God's perspective instead of the world's, and in so doing become more useful to God in the accomplishment of His purposes.

God-honoring attitudes are also *humbly submissive* to God's sovereign authority and will. Paul instructs us in Philippians 2:5–8 to imitate the attitude of Christ, who humbled Himself in obedience and submitted Himself to the Father's sovereign authority in order to accomplish God's will for mankind. Meditating on our Lord's willingness to disregard His equality with God as a thing to be grasped provides us with a convicting framework in which to sacrifice our own prideful desires and humbly submit ourselves to God's will for our lives.

Finally, God-honoring attitudes are *completely confident in God's provision*. Philippians 3:1–16 contains Paul's description of the ease with which he could have placed his ministerial confidence in the flesh instead of in the Lord, and the extent to which he went to avoid this temptation. He tells us that he counts these fleshly confidence builders as rubbish in view of the surpassing greatness of knowing the Lord Jesus Christ in the power of His resurrection and the fellowship of His sufferings. He then encourages his readers to have this same attitude and assures us that God will let us know when our attitudes go astray.

As we apply the truths of Scripture with the intent of taking our thoughts captive to the obedience of Christ, we should focus our attention on developing God-honoring attitudes that will free our behavior from ungodly motives.

## Doers of the Word

Meaningful application of Scripture requires thorough self-examination. We must not be afraid to analyze our thoughts, examine our attitudes, and evaluate our behavior biblically to determine what needs to be changed and then do what is necessary to bring about those changes. James 1:22–25 describes this process.

> Prove yourselves doers of the word, and not merely hearers who delude themselves. For if anyone is a hearer of the word and not a doer, he is like a man who looks at his natural face in a mirror; for once he has looked at himself and gone away, he has immediately forgotten what kind of person he was.
>
> But one who looks intently at the perfect law, the law of liberty, and abides by it, not having become a forgetful hearer but an effectual doer, this man shall be blessed in what he does.

The blessings associated with truly Christian living accrue to those who study the Word of God with the intent of conforming themselves to it. They search the Scriptures for teaching, reproof, correction, and training in righteousness. And they don't shy away from the necessity of change.

Most of us find it much easier to *identify* needed changes than to actually *make* those changes. How many times have you committed yourself to memorizing Scripture, studying the Bible daily, exercising regularly, or losing ten pounds, only to have all your good intentions evaporate in a few weeks? We usually fail to follow through on decisions like these because we fail to make a specific *plan of action* to carry them out. We know *what* we want to do but have no idea *how* we are going to do it.

The journalism questions we used in our observation of Scripture can help us develop a plan of action to implement change.

For example, let's say you need a plan to help you apply Philippians 2:3–4, about considering others more important than yourself. Ask yourself those six questions.

**Whom** will you consider more important than yourself? Pin it down to a person you can specifically identify. Let's suppose you decide to consider *your husband* more important than yourself. He travels all week, leaving you cooped up at home with kids, pets, and chores. By the time he gets home on Friday night, you are more than ready to drop the kids off at your mom's, lock the pets in the bathroom, forget the chores, and head for that great little Italian restaurant on the corner. Unfortunately, he has been eating in restaurants all week long and is looking forward to a home-cooked meal. Now, if you want to consider him more important than yourself . . .

**What** will you do for him? Cook his favorite meal.

**Where** will you do it? At home where he can kick off his shoes and relax.

**When** will you do it? Friday night.

**How** will you do it? Cheerfully.

**Why** will you do it? If you are thinking, "Well, if I fix him a good meal on Friday, then he will take me out on Saturday," you need to take another look at your attitude! The passage in Philippians doesn't teach that we should consider others more important than ourselves in order to be treated well in return.

If you cannot answer these six questions regarding scriptural applications that involve your behavior, your plan of action is not *specific* enough. Vague generalities don't generate change. Specific plans implemented in the power of the Holy Spirit do. Accountability also helps us implement change. Share your plan with a friend or relative who loves you enough to keep checking up on you.

You might also find it helpful to include all three aspects of application in your plan of action. Based on your study of the passage, consider what changes you need to make in your thought life, your attitudes, *and* your behavior. In applying Philippians 2:3–4, you may realize that you are harboring resentment against your husband because he is gone so much. Changing that *attitude* will require bringing your *thoughts* about your husband in line with Philippians 4:8.

# *Notes*

1. R. C. Sproul, *Knowing Scripture* (Downers Grove, Ill.: InterVarsity Press, 1977), 30.

# *Exercises*

## *Review*

1. Distinguish between subjectivism and subjectivity. Why is one inappropriate for Bible study while the other is essential?

2. Describe the importance of distinguishing between principles and application. Can you share a personal example regarding a time when failure to maintain this distinction created difficulty for you or someone you know?

3. Describe the three areas in which effective biblical change occurs.

4. What do Luke 1:17, Philippians 2:5–8, and Philippians 3:1–16 tell us about God-honoring attitudes?

5. Describe the relationship between attitude and obedience.

6. How does James's mirror analogy help you understand what it means to be a doer of the word?

7. Explain the benefits of developing a detailed plan of action for implementing biblical change. List several people who love you enough to hold you accountable to your plans to change.

## *Application*

1. Go through the passages from Ephesians and Colossians in appendix A again. Based on your observation and interpretation of these passages, make three *specific* applications to your own

life, one in the area of your *thinking,* one relating to your *attitudes,* and one directed toward your *behavior.* Make a detailed plan for implementing each application and commit yourself to a friend or relative who will hold you accountable to follow through on your applications.

2. Define the following words and phrases found in Philippians 4:8:

true:
honorable:
right:
pure:
lovely:
of good repute:
excellence:
worthy of praise:

Select a situation or a person you are currently having difficulty dealing with. Evaluate your thinking about this situation or person. Does your thinking coincide with the above definitions? If not, list the words and phrases from Philippians 4:8 on a three-by-five-inch index card, and next to each word or phrase, write a statement about this person or situation that fits the definition of that word or phrase. Carry this card with you for a period of six weeks. Each time this person or situation comes to mind, pull out the card, and concentrate on conforming your thinking in this area to Philippians 4:8. At the end of six weeks, determine if your *attitude* toward this person or situation has changed. If so, has your changed attitude affected your *behavior* toward this person or situation? Explain.

## Digging Deeper
1. In lesson 3 we described effective Bible study as a pyramid similar to the one used by nutritionists. Now that we have studied all three components of effective Bible study, see if you can explain in your own words why *much* observation is necessary

to produce *some* good solid interpretation, which in turn generates *a few* specific personal applications. In other words, why is a pyramid a better illustration of effective Bible study than a square or a circle?

2. In two columns, compare the Titus 2 woman (Titus 2:3–5) with the Proverbs 31 woman, applying everything you have learned so far about observation and interpretation. What do these passages have to do with you? Do you recognize yourself in the descriptions of these two women? Why or why not? What specific changes do you need to make in order to follow their example? How will you implement those changes? Who will hold you accountable?

# 7

# The Fruit of Bible Study

*Serious Bible study can make you pious or pompous, depending on your purpose for doing it. If you truly desire to know the Lord and walk worthy of your calling, serious Bible study will adequately equip you to become a pious follower. If you are more interested in impressing those around you with your vast knowledge of Scripture, serious Bible study will turn you into a pompous fool. The choice is yours.*

Serious Bible study produces two widely divergent groups of people: those who allow what they have learned to mold them into humble, submissive followers of Jesus Christ, and those who use what they have learned to inflate their egos. The difference can be understood by examining the purpose for which people undertake serious study.

John the Baptist and the apostle Paul were righteous students of the Scriptures who pursued learning with a godly purpose in mind. The Pharisees and Sadducees accumulated knowledge for purely selfish reasons. All of these men were involved in serious Bible study, but not all of them studied for the purpose of *following the Lord.*

*Why* we study the Bible is more important than *how* we study, and that is why this lesson appears at the end of our study instead of the beginning. Now that we have acquired some effective tools to help us understand God's Word, we must consciously submit our method of study to the overarching purpose of humbly following our Lord.

There are three primary study objectives that will keep us intent on our purpose: (1) Study with the intent of becoming conformed to the image of Christ; (2) study with the intent of glorifying God; and (3) study with the intent of building up the body of Christ.

## Conform to Christ's Image

The Westminster Shorter Catechism tells us that "man's chief end is to glorify God, and to enjoy him for ever." By placing the objective of conformity to the image of Christ ahead of the objective of glorifying God, I am in no way attempting to contradict that principle. What I *am* trying to do is demonstrate how important conformity to Christ's image is to the work of glorifying God. Believers simply cannot glorify God unless they are striving to become conformed to the image of Christ.

The Hebrew and Greek words for "glory" used in the Bible convey the idea of the majesty associated with God's self-revelation in His written Word and in His Son.[1] We glorify God by reflecting the majesty of His revealed attributes in our lives as we apply scriptural principles in order to become conformed to the image of Christ. Romans 8:28–29 tells us that God actively works all things together for good in the lives of believers because He predestined us "to become conformed to the image of His Son" so that we might glorify God in the world.

Becoming conformed to the image of Christ doesn't happen by osmosis, however. It requires effort and energy on our part. Ephesians 2:10 describes us as "His workmanship, created in Christ Jesus *for good works,* which God prepared beforehand, that we should walk in them." Becoming conformed to the image of Christ involves our participation in the good works God has prepared for us to do.

Scripture also reveals the ultimate purpose of the good works that conform us to the image of Christ. In Matthew 5:16, we read, "Let your light shine before men in such a way that they may see *your good works,* and *glorify your Father* who is in heaven."

As we work at becoming conformed to the image of Christ, we glorify God because we begin to think and behave in ways that reflect the indwelling Holy Spirit who mirrors Jesus Christ, who is the image of the invisible God and the exact representation of His nature. Thus the first objective of effective Bible study is to seek understanding of God's Word with the *intent* of using that understanding to become conformed to the image of Christ.

## Glorifying God

My favorite definition of glorifying God is "living your life in such a way that the people around you get a good idea of God's nature by looking at you." It's my favorite because it is so convicting. I live in the midst of unbelievers, none of whom read the Bible. Most of them know nothing about God, except what they see in me. I am not particularly comfortable living in that kind of fishbowl, but it has certainly kept me aware of my responsibility to glorify God in my daily life.

Glorifying God should be a routine part of our daily existence. We should glorify God by the way we prioritize our affairs and the way we spend our money. We should glorify God in the way we respond to His providential ordering of our circumstances and to the people He places in our paths. But we should also glorify God by including specific God-centered activities, such as the following, in our lives:

**Worship.** Jesus told the woman at the well that the Father seeks worshipers who will worship Him in spirit and truth. True worship necessarily exalts and extols the virtues of God and proceeds according to God's revealed will. Psalm 86:9–13 describes this kind of worship.

> All nations whom Thou hast made shall come and worship before Thee, O LORD;
> And they shall glorify Thy name.

For Thou art great and doest wondrous deeds;
Thou alone art God.
Teach me Thy way, O LORD;
I will walk in Thy truth;
Unite my heart to fear Thy name.
I will give thanks to Thee, O LORD my God, with all my
heart,
And will glorify Thy name forever.
For Thy lovingkindness toward me is great,
And Thou hast delivered my soul from the depths of Sheol.

**Prayer.** Prayer in Jesus' name provides the Father with an arena in which to display His power and wisdom. Jesus told His disciples, "Whatever you ask in My name, that will I do, that the Father may be glorified in the Son" (John 14:13).

**Service to Others.** God equips each of us to serve others by giving us special abilities beyond our natural talents to use in the furtherance of His kingdom. First Peter 4:10–11 describes how the exercise of these abilities glorifies God.

As each one has received a special gift, employ it in serving one another, as good stewards of the manifold grace of God. Whoever speaks, let him speak, as it were, the utterances of God; whoever serves, let him do so as by the strength which God supplies; so that in all things God may be glorified through Jesus Christ, to whom belongs the glory and dominion forever and ever.

**Confession of Sin.** One of the most dramatic demonstrations of the glory of God occurs when Christians openly confess and repent of their sin. There is no escaping the fact that unbelievers watch us sin, but that doesn't have to destroy our witness if they also watch us appropriate the grace of God promised in 1 John 1:9.

Perhaps the greatest testimony ever provided by repentance and confession was that of the apostle Paul. He describes this testimony in Galatians 1:11–24 when he mentions the reaction of the churches in Judea who kept hearing, "He who once persecuted us is now preaching the faith which he once tried to destroy" (v. 23). Paul says his turn-around was so great that "they were glorifying God because of me" (v. 24). When we allow the world to see God's gracious forgiveness and transforming power at work in our lives, we glorify Him.

**Suffering.** Suffering for the cause of Christ reveals the value we attach to our call to follow the Lord. When we stand firm regardless of the way we are treated, we glorify God magnificently. First Peter 4:14–16 describes this God-centered activity.

> If you are reviled for the name of Christ, you are blessed, because the Spirit of glory and of God rests upon you. By no means let any of you suffer as a murderer, or thief, or evildoer, or a troublesome meddler; but if anyone suffers as a Christian, let him not feel ashamed, but in that name let him glorify God.

**Evangelism.** Evangelism has been delightfully defined as declaring the gospel message clearly enough to allow the elect to accept it and the nonelect to reject it. Even though that definition is a bit simplistic, it captures the essence of all evangelistic effort—which is glorifying God regardless of the response to the message. When the gospel is clearly proclaimed, God's glory is displayed in the justification of those who believe and the condemnation of those who do not.

Ephesians 1 tells us that we were predestined to adoption as sons through Jesus Christ *to the praise of the glory of His grace,* that we who were the first to hope in Christ should be *to the praise of His glory,* and that the Holy Spirit of promise was given as a pledge of our inheritance *to the praise of His glory.* On the other hand, in the midst of God's condemnation of Sidon (Ezekiel 28) we read, "I shall be glorified in your midst. Then they will know that I am the LORD, when I execute judgments in her, and I shall manifest My holiness in her" (v. 22).

Effective Bible study calls us to apply what we learn with the conscious intent of glorifying God in everything we do.

## Building Up the Body of Christ

Effective Bible study also prepares us for the essential job of building up the body of Christ. Ephesians 4:11–13 describes the process through which the body of Christ matures and grows strong. God has appointed leaders for the church who equip the saints to do the work of ministry for the building up of the body of Christ. In a properly functioning body, the leaders concentrate on equipping the saints to perform ministry activities vital to the accomplishment of God's purposes. Every Christian woman operates within a unique sphere of influence that allows her to minister in ways no one else can.

Those of us who are mothers minister to and influence our children; those who teach Sunday school classes or youth groups minister to and influence other people's children. If you are an older woman, the younger women in your congregation look to you for guidance and wisdom. If you are single, childless, or widowed, you have time and energy at your disposal to invest in the lives of those around you. All of us influence others in one way or another, and if we are to influence them righteously, we ourselves must be properly equipped. And we cannot be properly equipped without participating in serious study of the Scriptures.

We can't teach others what we don't know ourselves. When young mothers tell me they don't have time for serious Bible study, I gently remind them of their responsibility to bring their children up in the discipline and instruction of the Lord. How can they teach their children what they have not taken the time to learn? Parents are primarily responsible to equip their children to serve God effectively, and in order to do that, *mothers* must know God's Word.

We also need to prepare ourselves to answer questions we are asked about our faith. First Peter 3:15–17 instructs us always to be prepared to give a defense (gently and respectfully) of the hope that we have. When your first grader wants to know why God doesn't have a wife, can you give her an answer from Scripture? When your teenager challenges you to explain what's wrong with premarital sex "if we're really in love," do you respond in anger, or with biblical wisdom? When your next-door neighbor asks you why she should believe the Bible and reject the Book of Mormon, can you give her an intelligent answer? Building up the body of

Christ (and potential members of the body) requires an ability to answer questions, and that ability is largely developed through effective Bible study.

Building up the body of Christ also requires us to set a godly example. The apostle Paul frequently encouraged his disciples to follow his example. Would you hesitate to do that? If so, why? Do your children know Bible study is important because they see you set aside a time each day, free from distractions, to focus on God's Word? Are your friends and relatives aware of your study habits? Would they become good students of the Bible if they followed your example?

### The Challenge of Serious Bible Study
Serious Bible study is a challenge that demands sacrifice. Accepting the challenge requires us to realign our priorities, reorganize our lives, and change firmly entrenched habits. It's a challenge we must not take lightly, but one we dare not refuse. How else can we righteously respond to our Lord who said to us, "If anyone wishes to come after Me, let him deny himself, and take up his cross, and follow Me. For whoever wishes to save his life shall lose it; but whoever loses his life for My sake and the gospel's shall save it. For what does it profit a man to gain the whole world, and forfeit his soul? For what shall a man give in exchange for his soul?" (Mark 8:34–37).

## Notes
1. Lawrence O. Richards, Expository Dictionary of Bible Words (Grand Rapids: Zondervan, 1985), 310–11.

## Exercises
### Review
1. Describe the two widely divergent groups of people produced by serious Bible study. What determines which group you will be in?

2. List three objectives for Bible study that will help you maintain a godly purpose for study. Can you think of any others?

3. Why is striving to become conformed to the image of Christ necessary for believers to glorify God?

4. Describe some ways we can glorify God in our daily routine.

5. Explain how each of the following activities should glorify God:

   worship:
   prayer:
   service to others:
   confession of sin:
   suffering:
   evangelism:

   How might each of these activities be done in a way that does *not* glorify God?

6. Why should *all* Christians be concerned with building up the body of Christ?

## Application

1. Explain how your study of the passages from Ephesians and Colossians in appendix A will help you do the following: (Remember to be *very specific* in your answers! No vague generalities, please.)

   become conformed to the image of Christ:
   glorify God:
   build up the body of Christ:

2. You met the following women in lesson 1 and responded to their reasons for not accepting the challenge of serious Bible study. Read their reasons again and see if you would respond

to them differently now that you have almost completed this study.

**Sylvia's reason:**
"Frankly, I don't have the time. With four children under the age of ten and a husband who works fifty hours a week, I'm lucky to get a few minutes a day to read a few verses and say a quick prayer. Maybe when the children are older . . . but right now, serious Bible study is out of the question."

**Lynda's reason:**
"My husband is the head of our house and my high priest. He does all the Bible study and determines what our family will believe. My job is to follow his lead without question and support his decisions. Studying the Bible on my own would only confuse me and make it harder for me to follow his leadership."

**Stephanie's reason:**
"I read the Bible every day and it means so much to me. I experience the most wonderful feelings of peace and contentment when I read God's Word, and I don't want to lose that. I am afraid if I start studying the Bible like a subject in school, it will become nothing more than an academic exercise instead of the profound emotional experience it is now."

**Tanya's reason:**
"I go to a wonderful church and my pastor has spent years studying the Bible. He is a truly gifted teacher who explains the Bible so well. I know I could never study the Bible as well as he does, so I am content to just let him teach me."

**Cynthia's reason:**
"I would like to, but I have no idea how to do it."

**Rita's reason:**
"I'm not sure the Bible is reliable. Some of those stories are pretty fantastic and sound more like myths and fairy tales than facts, and I'm not one to base my life on myths and fairy tales."

*The Fruit of Bible Study*

**Karin's reason:**

"I do study the Bible, and I love it. I'm just not sure I am coming up with the right answers. There are so many Bible teachers and scholars who disagree on what different parts of the Bible mean. How do I know I am believing the right things?"

**Helen's reason:**

"Jesus is my Savior and He is all I need. I pray every day and listen for His voice. I depend on the Holy Spirit to guide me in everything I do. The Bible doesn't speak to me the way His Spirit does, so I don't pay much attention to it."

**Diana's reason:**

"I used to study the Bible, and I felt guilty all the time. It got to where I couldn't take it anymore, and I feel much better since I quit."

Sylvia:

Lynda:

Stephanie:

Tanya:

Cynthia:

Rita:

Karin:

Helen:

Diana:

Has your willingness to accept the challenge of serious Bible study changed as a result of completing this study? Explain.

3. If you are ready to accept the challenge of serious Bible study, record your commitment in writing. You may write a paragraph, compose a song or a poem, address a letter to God, or choose some other creative way of stating this commitment. Share your commitment with someone who loves you enough to hold you accountable, and ask him or her to help you remain faithful to your commitment.

78

## Digging Deeper

1. Study Ephesians 4:11–16. If you are a young woman with children entrusted to your care, explain how these verses will help you equip your children to serve God effectively. If you are an older woman with grown children, explain how these verses impact your relationship with younger women in the body of Christ. If you are a single woman or have no children, explain how these verses speak to your influence on those around you.

2. Use some creative method to demonstrate the difference between those who become pious followers of Jesus Christ as a result of serious Bible study and those who become pompous fools as a result of serious Bible study. (Compose a poem or song, draw a picture, write a short story or a play. Be imaginative but make a biblical point.)

# Readings from
# Ephesians and Colossians

*Several application exercises call for reading and reflecting on the following passages. Extra line and margin space is provided here to allow you to make marks and notations on insights gleaned from these readings.*

## *Ephesians 4:1–7; 4:17–5:2; 5:15–6:9; 6:18–20*

I, therefore, the prisoner of the Lord, entreat you to walk

in a manner worthy of the calling with which you have

been called, with all humility and gentleness, with pa-

tience, showing forbearance to one another in love, being

diligent to preserve the unity of the Spirit in the bond of

peace. There is one body and one Spirit, just as also you

were called in one hope of your calling; one Lord, one faith,

one baptism, one God and Father of all who is over all and

through all and in all. But to each one of us grace was given according to the measure of Christ's gift. . . .

This I say therefore, and affirm together with the Lord, that you walk no longer just as the Gentiles also walk, in the futility of their mind, being darkened in their understanding, excluded from the life of God, because of the ignorance that is in them, because of the hardness of their heart; and they, having become callous, have given themselves over to sensuality, for the practice of every kind of impurity with greediness. But you did not learn Christ in this way, if indeed you have heard Him and have been taught in Him, just as truth is in Jesus, that, in reference to your former manner of life, you lay aside the old self, which is being corrupted in accordance with the lusts of deceit, and that you be renewed in the spirit of your mind, and put on the new self, which in the likeness of God has been created in righteousness and holiness of the truth.

Therefore, laying aside falsehood, speak truth, each one

of you, with his neighbor, for we are members of one another. Be angry, and yet do not sin; do not let the sun go down on your anger, and do not give the devil an opportunity. Let him who steals steal no longer; but rather let him labor, performing with his own hands what is good, in order that he may have something to share with him who has need. Let no unwholesome word proceed from your mouth, but only such a word as is good for edification according to the need of the moment, that it may give grace to those who hear. And do not grieve the Holy Spirit of God, by whom you were sealed for the day of redemption. Let all bitterness and wrath and anger and clamor and slander be put away from you, along with all malice. And be kind to one another, tender-hearted, forgiving each other, just as God in Christ also has forgiven you.

Therefore be imitators of God, as beloved children; and walk in love, just as Christ also loved you, and gave Himself up for us, an offering and a sacrifice to God as a fragrant aroma. . . .

Therefore be careful how you walk, not as unwise men, but as wise, making the most of your time, because the days are evil. So then do not be foolish, but understand what the will of the Lord is. And do not get drunk with wine, for that is dissipation, but be filled with the Spirit, speaking to one another in psalms and hymns and spiritual songs, singing and making melody with your heart to the Lord; always giving thanks for all things in the name of our Lord Jesus Christ to God, even the Father; and be subject to one another in the fear of Christ.

Wives, be subject to your own husbands, as to the Lord. For the husband is the head of the wife, as Christ also is the head of the church, He Himself being the Savior of the body. But as the church is subject to Christ, so also the wives ought to be to their husbands in everything. Husbands, love your wives, just as Christ also loved the church and gave Himself up for her; that He might sanctify her, having cleansed her by the washing of water by the word, that He might present to Himself the church in all her glory, having no spot or wrinkle or any such thing; but that she should be holy

and blameless. So husbands ought also to love their own

wives as their own bodies. He who loves his own wife loves

himself; for no one ever hated his own flesh, but nourishes

and cherishes it, just as Christ also does the church, because

we are members of His body. For this cause a man shall

leave his father and mother, and shall cleave to his wife; and

the two shall become one flesh. This mystery is great; but

I am speaking with reference to Christ and the church.

Nevertheless let each individual among you also love his

own wife even as himself; and let the wife see to it that she

respect her husband.

Children, obey your parents in the Lord, for this is right.

Honor your father and mother (which is the first com-

mandment with a promise), that it may be well with you,

and that you may live long on the earth. And, fathers, do

not provoke your children to anger; but bring them up in

the discipline and instruction of the Lord.

Slaves, be obedient to those who are your masters according to the flesh, with fear and trembling, in the sincerity of your heart, as to Christ; not by way of eyeservice, as men-pleasers, but as slaves of Christ, doing the will of God from the heart. With good will render service, as to the Lord, and not to men, knowing that whatever good thing each one does, this he will receive back from the Lord, whether slave or free. And, masters, do the same things to them, and give up threatening, knowing that both their Master and yours is in heaven, and there is no partiality with Him. . . .

With all prayer and petition pray at all times in the Spirit, and with this in view, be on the alert with all perseverance and petition for all the saints, and pray on my behalf, that utterance may be given to me in the opening of my mouth, to make known with boldness the mystery of the gospel, for which I am an ambassador in chains; that in proclaiming it I may speak boldly, as I ought to speak.

## Colossians 3:1–4:6

If then you have been raised up with Christ, keep seeking the things above, where Christ is, seated at the right hand of God. Set your mind on the things above, not on the things that are on earth. For you have died and your life is hidden with Christ in God. When Christ, who is our life, is revealed, then you also will be revealed with Him in glory.

Therefore consider the members of your earthly body as dead to immorality, impurity, passion, evil desire, and greed, which amounts to idolatry. For it is on account of these things that the wrath of God will come, and in them you also once walked, when you were living in them. But now you also, put them all aside: anger, wrath, malice, slander, and abusive speech from your mouth. Do not lie to one another, since you laid aside the old self with its evil practices, and have put on the new self who is being renewed to a true knowledge according to the image of the One who created him—a renewal in which there is no distinction between Greek and Jew, circumcised and uncircumcised, barbarian, Scythian, slave and freeman, but Christ is all, and in all.

And so, as those who have been chosen of God, holy and beloved, put on a heart of compassion, kindness, humility, gentleness, and patience; bearing with one another, and forgiving each other, whoever has a complaint against anyone; just as the Lord forgave you, so also should you. And beyond all these things put on love, which is the perfect bond of unity. And let the peace of Christ rule in your hearts, to which indeed you were called in one body; and be thankful. Let the word of Christ richly dwell within you, with all wisdom teaching and admonishing one another with psalms and hymns and spiritual songs, singing with thankfulness in your hearts to God. And whatever you do in word or deed, do all in the name of the Lord Jesus, giving thanks through Him to God the Father.

Wives, be subject to your husbands, as is fitting in the Lord. Husbands, love your wives, and do not be embittered against them. Children, be obedient to your parents in all things, for this is well-pleasing to the Lord. Fathers, do not exasperate your children, that they may not lose heart. Slaves, in all things obey those who are your masters on earth, not with external service, as those who merely please men, but with sincerity of heart, fearing the Lord. Whatever you do, do your work heartily, as for the Lord rather than for men; knowing that from the Lord you will receive the reward of the inheritance. It is the Lord Christ whom you serve. For he who does wrong will receive the consequences of the wrong which he has done, and that without partiality.

Masters, grant to your slaves justice and fairness, knowing that you too have a Master in heaven.

Devote yourselves to prayer, keeping alert in it with an attitude of thanksgiving; praying at the same time for us as well, that God may open up to us a door for the word, so that we may speak forth the mystery of Christ, for which I have also been imprisoned; in order that I may make it clear in the way I ought to speak. Conduct your-

selves with wisdom toward outsiders, making the most of

the opportunity. Let your speech always be with grace, sea-

soned, as it were, with salt, so that you may know how

you should respond to each person.

## APPENDIX B

# Supplemental Exercises

Every time I become involved in a Bible study, there seem to be a few people who never get enough. They do all the homework each week and wish there were more! If you fall into that category, this section is for you. The following exercises will provide you with several challenging opportunities to apply to a variety of topics what you have learned in this study. I hope you enjoy them.

1. Study Romans 6 and explain why Christians continue to sin after they are saved if sin is no longer master over them. (Hint: You will probably find it very helpful to read chapters 5–8 to put chapter 6 in context.)

2. Based on your study of Romans 6, respond to the following statements sometimes made by professing Christians:

> "Overcoming sin is impossible. The Christian life is a war. My old nature and my new nature are constantly battling, and the one that happens to be stronger on a particular day determines my behavior."

> "When I became a Christian, Satan's control over my life was broken once and for all. If I discipline myself to obey God, I can overcome sin and eventually reach a stage of perfection in this life. I can refrain from sinning if I want to badly enough. The only excuses for continuing to sin are ignorance of God's commands and/or laziness."

3. Read through the book of Jude keeping in mind the purpose statement found in verse 3. See if you can detect the *themes* of the book of Jude, and try to outline the book around those themes.

4. Read through the book of Philemon. What is Paul's purpose for writing this book, and what are the main themes of the book? What kind of historical insights might help you better understand the book of Philemon?

5. Read quickly through the books of Galatians and Philippians, and see if you can detect a difference in Paul's *attitude* toward these two groups of people. Which words or phrases give you clues to his attitude?

6. Using a concordance and any other reliable study aids available to you, study the subject of election as it is taught in Scripture. (In addition to the word *election,* you will also want to look at words like *predestined, called,* and *chosen.*) When you have completed your study, respond to this statement made by John MacArthur, Jr., in his commentary on Colossians:

> The doctrine of election crushes human pride, exalts God, produces joy and gratitude to the Lord, grants eternal privileges and assurance, promises holiness, and makes one bold and courageous, for one who has been chosen by God for eternal life has no need to fear anything or anyone.

7. Many Christians use the following verses to support their belief that a genuine believer can either lose or forfeit his salvation: Galatians 5:4; Hebrews 6:4–6; Hebrews 10:26–27; and 2 Peter 3:17. (If you are aware of other verses used to support this position, include them in the list.) Using your current knowledge of Scripture and the study skills you have learned in this class, supplemented by as many good study aids as you can access, determine if this interpretation can be supported in the context of the

entire Bible. Try your best to divorce yourself from your own theological preferences and let Scripture interpret Scripture.

8. The word *justify* is used in Scripture to mean (1) to restore to a state of reconciliation with God those who are under condemnation, or (2) to demonstrate or vindicate. Use a concordance to locate passages of Scripture in which Paul uses this word and in which James uses the word. Study these passages in context and in light of the whole counsel of God and determine if Paul and James contradict each other in their teaching. Explain your conclusions.

9. Using a concordance, a Bible dictionary, and any other reliable study tools available to you, do some research on the word *glory*. Look up the Hebrew and Greek words translated "glory" and study their meanings and their usage. Study the glory of God in the Old and New Testaments and the ways we are instructed to glorify Him. Based on your study, do you believe the definition of glorifying God on page 71 is a good one? Why or why not? Write your own definition of glorifying God, if you like, and explain how it will help you maintain a godly focus in your study of Scripture.

10. Creatively illustrate the statement from the Westminster Shorter Catechism, "Man's chief end is to glorify God, and to enjoy him for ever." (Draw a picture, compose a song, write a poem or short story, prepare a dramatic reading or a collage. See how creative you can be in depicting this profound truth.)

# APPENDIX C

# What Must I Do to Be Saved?

A strange sound drifted through the Philippian jail as midnight approached. The sound of human voices—but not the expected groans of the two men who had earlier been beaten with rods and fastened in stocks. Rather, the peaceful singing of praises to their God.

While the other prisoners quietly listened to them, the jailer dozed off, content with the bizarre calm generated by these two preachers, who, hours before, had stirred up so much commotion in the city.

Suddenly a deafening roar filled the prison as the ground began to shake violently. Sturdy doors convulsed and popped open. Chains snapped and fell at prisoners' feet. Startled into full wakefulness, the jailer stared at the wide-open doors and realized his prisoners' certain escape guaranteed his own impending death. Under Roman law, jailers paid with their lives when prisoners escaped. Resolutely, he drew his sword, thinking it better to die by his own hand than by Roman execution.

"Stop! Don't harm yourself—we are all here!" a voice boomed from the darkened inner cell. The jailer called for lights and was astonished to discover his prisoners standing quietly amid their broken chains. Trembling, he rushed in and fell at the feet of the two preachers. As soon as he was able, he led them out of the prison and asked, "Sirs, what must I do to be saved?"

In the entire history of the world, no one has ever asked a more important question. The jailer's words that night may well have been motivated by his critical physical need, but the response of Paul and Silas addressed his even more critical spiritual need: "Believe in the Lord Jesus, and you shall be saved, you and your household" (Acts 16:31).[1]

If you have never "believed in the Lord Jesus," your spiritual need, just like the jailer's, is critical. As long as your life is stained with sin, God cannot receive you into His presence. The Bible says that sin has placed a separation between you and God (Isaiah 59:2). It goes on to say that your nature has been so permeated by sin that you no longer have any desire to serve and obey God (Romans 3:10–12); therefore, you are not likely to recognize or care that a separation exists. Your situation is truly desperate because those who are separated from God will spend eternity in hell.

Since sinful hearts are unresponsive to God, the only way sinners can be saved from their desperate situation is for God to take the initiative. And this He has done! Even though all men and women deserve the punishment of hell because of their sin, God's love has prompted Him to save some who will serve Him in obedience. He did this by sending His Son, the Lord Jesus Christ, to remove the barrier of sin between God and His chosen ones (Colossians 2:13–14).

What is there about Jesus that enables Him to do this? First of all, He is God. While He was on earth, He said, "He who has seen Me has seen the Father" (John 14:9), and "I and the Father are one" (John 10:30). Because He said these things, you must conclude one of three things about His true identity: (1) He was a lunatic who believed He was God when He really wasn't; (2) He was a liar who was willing to die a hideous death for what He knew was a lie; or (3) His words are true and He is God.

Lunatics don't live the way Jesus did, and liars don't die the way He did, so if the Bible's account of Jesus' life and words is true, you can be sure He *is* God.

Since Jesus is God, He is perfectly righteous and holy. God's perfect righteousness and holiness demands that sin be punished (Ezekiel 18:4), and Jesus' perfect righteousness and holiness qualified Him to bear the punishment for the sins of those who will be saved (Romans 6:23). Jesus is the only human who never committed a sin; therefore, the punishment He bore when He died on the cross could be accepted by God as satisfaction of His justice in regard to the sins of others.

If someone you love commits a crime and is sentenced to die, you may offer to die in his place. However, if you have also committed crimes worthy of death, your death cannot satisfy the law's demands for your crimes *and* your loved one's. You can only die in his place if you are innocent of any wrongdoing.

Since Jesus lived a perfect life, God's justice could be satisfied by allowing Him to die for the sins of those who will be saved. Because God is perfectly righteous and holy, He could not act in love at the expense of justice. By sending Jesus to die, God demonstrated His love *by acting to satisfy His own justice* (Romans 3:26).

Jesus did more than die, however. He also rose from the dead. By raising Jesus from the dead, God declared that He had accepted Jesus' death in the place of those who will be saved. Because Jesus lives eternally with God, those for whom Jesus died can be assured they will also spend eternity in heaven (John 14:1–3). The separation of sin has been removed!

Ah, but the all-important question remains unanswered: What must *you do* to be saved? If God has sent His Son into the world for sinners, and Jesus Christ has died in their place, what is left for you to do? You must respond in faith to what God has done. This is what Paul meant when he told the jailer, "Believe in the Lord Jesus, and you shall be saved."

Believing in the Lord Jesus demands three responses from you: (1) an understanding of the facts regarding your hopeless sinful condition and God's action to remove the sin barrier that separates you from Him; (2) acceptance of those facts as true and applicable to you; and (3) a willingness to trust and depend upon God to save you from sin. This involves willingly placing yourself under His authority and acknowledging His sovereign right to rule over you.

But, you say, how can I do this if sin has eliminated my ability to know and appreciate God's work on my behalf? Rest assured that if you desire to have the sin barrier that separates you from God removed, He is already working to change your natural inability to respond. He is extending His gracious offer of salvation to you and will give you the faith to receive it.

If you believe God is working to call you to Himself, read the words He has written to you in the Bible (begin with the book of John in the New Testament) and pray that His Holy Spirit will help you understand what is written there. Continue to read and pray until you are ready to *repent,* that is, to turn away from sin and commit yourself to serving God.

Is there any other way you can be saved? God Himself says no, there is not. The Bible He wrote says that Jesus is the only way the sin barrier between you and God can be removed (John 14:6; Acts 4:12). He is your hope, and He is your *only* hope.

If you have questions or need any help in this matter, please write to The Evangelism Team, Providence Presbyterian Church, P. O. Box 14651, Albuquerque, NM 87191, before the day is over. God has said in His Bible that a day of judgment is coming, and after that day no one will be saved (Acts 17:30–31; 2 Thessalonians 1:7–9). The time to act is now.

## *Notes*

1. See Acts 16:11–40 for the full biblical account of these events.

# APPENDIX D

# What Is the Reformed Faith?

"The Reformed faith"[1] can be defined as a theology that describes and explains the sovereign God's revelation of His actions in history to glorify Himself by redeeming selected men and women from the just consequences of their self-inflicted depravity.

It is first and foremost *theology* (the study of God), not *anthropology* (the study of humanity). Reformed thinking concentrates on developing a true knowledge of God that serves as the necessary context for all other knowledge. It affirms that the created world, including humanity itself, cannot be accurately understood apart from its relationship with the Creator.

The Reformed faith describes and explains God's revelation of Himself and His actions to humanity; it does not consist of people's attempts to define God as they wish. The Reformed faith asserts that God has revealed Himself in two distinct ways. He reveals His existence, wisdom, and power through the created universe—a process known as *natural revelation* (Romans 1:18–32); and He reveals His requirements and plans for mankind through His written Word, the Bible—a process known as *special revelation* (2 Timothy 3:16–17).

Reformed theologians uphold the Bible as the inspired, infallible, inerrant, authoritative, and fully sufficient communication of truth from God to us. When they say the Bible is "inspired," they mean that the Bible was actually written by God through the agency of human authorship in a miraculous way that preserved the thoughts of God from any taint of human sinfulness (2 Peter 1:20–21).

When they say the Bible is infallible, they mean it is *incapable* of error, and when they say it is inerrant, they mean the Bible, *in actual fact,* contains no errors. The Bible is authoritative because it comes from God whose authority over His creation is absolute (Isaiah 46:9–10). And it is completely sufficient because it contains everything necessary for us to know and live according to God's requirements (2 Peter 1:3–4).

By studying God's revelation of Himself and His work, Reformed theologians have learned two foundational truths that structure their thinking about God's relationship with human beings: God is absolutely sovereign, and people are totally depraved.[2]

Reformed thought affirms that God, by definition, is *absolutely sovereign*—that is, He controls and superintends every circumstance of life either by direct miraculous intervention or by the ordinary outworking of His providence. Reformed theologians understand that a "god" who is not sovereign cannot be God because his power would not be absolute. Since the Reformed faith accepts the Bible's teaching regarding the sovereignty of God, it denies that *anything* occurs outside of God's control.

The Reformed faith affirms the biblical teaching that Adam was created with the ability to sin and chose to do so by disobeying a clear command of God (Genesis 3:1–7). Choosing to sin changed basic human nature and left us unable not to sin—or *totally depraved.* Total depravity does not mean that all people are as bad as they possibly could be, but that every facet of their character is tainted with sin, leaving them incapable and undesirous of fellowship with God. The Reformed faith denies that totally depraved men and women have any ability to seek after or submit to God of their own free will. Left to themselves, totally depraved men and women will remain out of fellowship with God for all eternity.

The only way for any of these men and women to have their fellowship with God restored is for God Himself to take the initiative. And the Bible declares that He has graciously chosen to do so (John 14:16). *For His own glory,* God has chosen some of those depraved men and women to live in fellowship with Him. His choice is determined by His own good pleasure and not by any virtue in the ones He has chosen. For this reason, *grace* is defined in Reformed thought as "unmerited favor."

God accomplished the salvation of His chosen ones by sending His Son, the Lord Jesus Christ, to bear God's righteous wrath against sin so that He could forgive those He had chosen. Even though Christ's work was perfect and complete, its effectiveness is limited to those who are chosen by God for salvation. Christ would not have been required to suffer any more or any less had a different number been chosen for redemption, but the benefit of His suffering is applied only to those who are called by God to believe in Him.

All of those who are thus effectually called by God will eventually believe and be saved, even though they may resist for a time (John 6:37). They cannot forfeit the salvation they have received (John 10:27–30; Romans 8:31–39).

Reformed thought affirms the clear teaching of the Bible that salvation is by faith alone through Christ alone (John 14:6; Acts 4:12; Ephesians 2:8–9), and that our good works play no part in salvation although they are generated by it (Ephesians 2:10). Salvation transforms a person's nature, giving him or her the ability and the desire to serve and obey God. The unresponsive heart of stone is changed into a sensitive heart of flesh that responds readily to God's voice (Ezekiel 36:25–27) and desires to glorify Him out of gratitude for the indescribable gift of salvation.

Reformed thought affirms that *God works in history to redeem* His chosen ones through a series of covenants. These covenants define His law, assess penalties for breaking His law, and provide for the imputation of Jesus' vicarious fulfillment of God's requirements to those God intends to redeem.[3]

The Reformed faith affirms that we were created and exist solely to glorify God, and denies that God exists to serve us. It affirms that God acts to glorify Himself by putting His attributes on display, and that His self-glorifying actions are thoroughly righteous since He is the only Being in creation worthy of glorification. It denies that God is *primarily* motivated to act by man's needs, but affirms that all of God's actions are motivated *primarily* for His own glory.

The Reformed faith emerged as a distinct belief system during the sixteenth and seventeenth centuries when men like Luther, Calvin, Zwingli, and Knox fought against the Roman Catholic

Church to restore Christian doctrine to biblical truth. These men were labeled "Reformers," but they would have been better labeled "Restorers" since their goal was to correct abuses and distortions of Christianity that were rampant in the established Roman church. Reformed thinkers since their day have sought to align their understanding of God and His actions in history as closely as possible to His revealed truth.

# Notes

1. This brief overview of basic Reformed beliefs is not intended to be a full explanation of or apologetic for the Reformed faith. For a more detailed description and analysis of the Reformed faith see: R. C. Sproul, *Grace Unknown* (Grand Rapids: Baker, 1997), Loraine Boettner, *The Reformed Faith* (Phillipsburg, N.J.: Presbyterian and Reformed, 1983), *Back to Basics: Rediscovering the Richness of the Reformed Faith,* ed. David G. Hagopian (Phillipsburg, N.J.: P&R Publishing, 1996), *The Westminster Confession of Faith* (with its accompanying catechisms), or the theological writings of John Calvin, B. B. Warfield, Charles Hodge, and Louis Berkhof.

2. Both of these truths are taught throughout the pages of Scripture; however, the sovereignty of God can be seen very clearly in Isaiah 40–60 and in Job 38–42, while human depravity is described quite graphically in Romans 3:10–18.

3. An excellent discussion of these covenants is contained in chapter 5 of R. C. Sproul, *Grace Unknown.*

# RECOMMENDED READING

Adler, Mortimer J., and Charles Van Doren. *How to Read a Book.* New York: Simon and Schuster, 1972.

Berkhof, Louis. *Principles of Biblical Interpretation.* Grand Rapids: Baker, 1950.

Doriani, Daniel M. *Getting the Message: A Plan for Interpreting and Applying the Bible.* Phillipsburg, N.J.: P&R Publishing, 1996.

Hendricks, Howard G., and William D. Hendricks. *Living by the Book.* Chicago: Moody Press, 1991.

Jensen, Irving L. *Independent Bible Study.* Chicago: Moody Press, 1963.

McDowell, Josh. *Evidence That Demands a Verdict.* San Bernadino: Here's Life Publishers, 1972, 1979.

Robertson, O. Palmer. *Understanding the Land of the Bible: A Biblical-Theological Guide.* Phillipsburg, N.J.: P&R Publishing, 1996.

Sproul, R. C. *Knowing Scripture.* Downers Grove, Ill.: InterVarsity Press, 1977.